DON'T EAT ME!

A Cookbook for Animal Lovers

by Robin Gager

L B

Late Bloomers Publishing
Larchmont, NY

D1515563

DON'T EAT ME! A Cookbook For Animal Lovers

Text Copyright © 2009 Robin Gager
Food Photography Copyright © 2009 Denise Chastain Photography

Published by
Late Bloomers Publishing
P.O. Box 2035
Larchmont, NY 10538
www.donteatme.org

12 09 09 08

ISBN-13: 978-0-615-34230-6
ISBN-10: 0615342302

Library of Congress Cataloging-in-Publication Data
Gager, Robin.
DON'T EAT ME! A Cookbook For Animal Lovers/ Robin Gager.
p. cm.
Includes Index.
ISBN 0615342302

Cover photo and specified internal photos by Derek Goodwin
Cover and book design by Robin Gager and Christen Napier
Animal photography in chapter headings by Robin Gager
"Compassion Sign" artwork by Jean Rhode
Bumper sticker illustration by Alysha Auslender
Edited by Diane Gager-Hesler

Printed and bound in South Korea

Contents

In Memory of
Kenneth E. Sparacino, Jr.

A beautiful soul, a great songwriter, a dear friend
who taught me and everyone who knew him that
it's never too late to become a vegetarian.

Acknowledgements

This book has been a labor of love that has never felt like real labor at all. In fact, working on this book, has been, by far, one of the best experiences of my life. To go on such a journey with so many amazingly talented, generous, and supportive people is something for which I know I am unbelievably blessed. Every single person who donated their time and efforts to this book did so out of the goodness of their heart, and with great enthusiasm, because they believed in this book and what it stands for. If that isn't incredibly special, I don't know what is.

I would first like to thank all my friends and family who have been so genuinely enthusiastic. Thanks for your support. I love you guys!

I would like to thank my brother, Brian Gager, for introducing me to the Woodstock Farm Animal Sanctuary, which was meant to be the focal point that this book revolves around all along. To everyone at the Woodstock Farm Animal Sanctuary, I take my hat off to you, and the tremendous work that you do everyday.

Thank you to Rebecca Moore, my very helpfull liason at WFAS who seems to have made it her own personal mission to assist me. Thank you to Jenny Brown and Doug Abel, the co-founders of WFAS, for donating key pictures to the book, and for finding the time to help me out when I needed you, even though you already have so much on your own plate! Thank you to Julie Goodloe and Amber Plaut, who participated in my photo shoots and allowed me to use their pictures in the book.

Much thanks to Jean Rhode for allowing me to use her beautiful compassion sign artwork that appears in the kids menu, and especially to Derek Goodwin for taking the fantastic cover photo of baby Dylan that I just fell in love with. Many thanks for letting us use it, and the other WFAS pictures of Jenny and Doug, Dylan and Julie, and Jenny and Dylan. And of course, thank you to my farm animal friends who grace the pages of this book: Sheila the chicken, Dylan the cow, the piglets, Pinky and Eva, Celia the sheep, and all the rest of the crew! Xoxoxoxoxo.

To everyone who donated a recipe to the book; I can't thank you enough. Your creations are the missing pieces of the puzzle that make this book whole. Steven Bowe, I hardly know you, but I know that you can cook, and that's for sure! Your rice pudding is like a dream come true. To my dear Christen Napier, you know I now live on tofu scramble thanks to you. And Brian Gager, my brother, you make a mean portobello burger.

To my mom and dad (known to the world as Dolly and Stew Gager), people might think at first glance that I put your no-sausage stuffed acorn squash, and your french onion soup in this book just because you are members of my family, but they will soon see that I learned to cook, and appreciate really good food, from you. I always tell everyone, that I grew up eating in the best restaurant around; my own home.

To my friend Lucy Close: not only did you bail me out with your delicious I'll Be Home for Christmas Roast, but you totally saved the day by investing in the cookbook when I didn't know where else to turn. Thank you for your generosity, and for your unwavering belief and trust in me.

A special thank you to John Andriani, who has been along for the ride of this cookbook, before I even called it a cookbook, and who has definitely tasted more of my recipes than anyone. He is a friend who has supported me greatly, and who is a very good cook himself (his tofu-no meatballs, with his quick and juicy marinara should be on your bucket-list). I must also truly thank him for introducing me to my awesomely talented photographer, Denise Chastain, and for his steadfast devotion to the New York Mets, which ultimately led to the birth of this cookbook. (Long story.) Let's go Mets!

I can't imagine this book without Bill Glasser's magnificent, show-stopping, Topanga Thanksgiving No-Turkey. I plan on eating it every Thanksgiving for the rest of my life! And I must thank Bill's mother, Deb Glasser, without whom I would never have known about Bill, or his amazing creation, which I am so lucky to have in my book.

To all my friends who participated in the photo-shoots; you are the ones who bring this book to life. I love looking through it, and seeing your beautiful faces! To the Stanton Family; Maria, Greg, Isobella, Luke and Nina, who have always been so kind to me, and to the Kennedy/Schweizer family; Michelle Kennedy, Greg Schweizer, Devon Jane Schweizer and Korben Schweizer, and to Judith Stuck and Maxwell Kalba; Thank you so much for trucking all the way up to The WoodStock Farm Sanctuary for me, and hanging in there on that miserable, cold, and rainy day. You guys were serious troopers, and because of your commitment, and true-grit, we got some of the best pictures in the book!

Warm thanks to my friend Sharon Cook, who appears in the no-killin grillin section, and whose wisdom, positive attitude, and helping hand has helped save me from a nervous breakdown on more than one photo shoot. Thanks for giving of yourself so generously as you always do! And to Robert Ferraro, who was such an amazing sport so many countless times. Thank you for taking on your role as the token guy, that we volunteered you for, with such enthusiasm and great wit, and for letting me and my friends, invade your and Denise's house on so many, many occasions. You rock!

To everyone involved in the marathon known as the Chanukah/Thanksgiving/Christmas shoot, all I can say is that every last one of you is a super-hero! I feel like we accomplished the impossible that night, with many of us teetering on the verge of utter collapse. But we did it!!!!!! To Matthew Burcaw, for braving the Friday night traffic to Long Island; Benjamin Pequet, for force-feeding himself through Chanukah AND Thanksgiving, and Janira Campos for being such a great actress, I salute you! To Judith and Maureen Stuck, and Sherry St. Pierre; your picture with Santa is a classic! Robert Ferraro, once again, you made it into the centerpiece with your surreal carving of the no-turkey!

To my biggest little stars: Daniela and Chris St. Pierre, thanks for being a part of my book, and doing such a great job! and Maxwell Kalba. I don't think a potato latke has ever been stared at with such intensity! You guys stole the show! Speaking of stars, I would also like to thank my young taste-tester, Sophia Schöenau, for giving me such great feedback for the kids menu.

No one has ever gotten anywhere in life without a leg-up from someone. I especially want to thank everyone who has gone out on a limb to try and find this book a publisher: My friend Stephanie Nieuwjaer, my sweet neighbors, Maria Lovoce and Rose Falco. David Sweeney at HarperCollins Publishing, for his time and encouragement,

Dan Piraro, for advising me to contact Martin Rowe at Lantern Books, and Martin Rowe himself. Also, thank you to my good friend Lucy Close who seems to be everywhere at once, and my mom, Dolly Gager, for encouraging me to self-publish this book.

And now, to the wonderful women who are the backbone of this book; my own personal dream team: this book would be a fraction of what it is without you. Thank you to Liz Squillace, who worked on the artwork for the first cover concept before we changed it. To my friend and co-worker, Alysha Auslender, who created the incredibly adorable, and perfect cartoon characters for the donteatme.org bumpersticker: to think that I was looking for a cartoonist for over a year, and you were right under my nose the entire time! And so funny that I asked you if you knew any cartoonists and your first response was to recommend me to someone else! Good God girl! You are too modest, but that is part of your charm. Thank you for being so selfless in your intention to help animals, and for creating such great characters for the book. I know they will make a big impression on people, and that's what it's all about!!!!

To my beautiful cousin Diane Gager Hesler, who volunteered herself for the enormous, time-consuming, needle in a haystack job of editing this entire book, not once, but twice, all I can say is I have adored you all my life, and it is so special to be working on a project that is so dear to me with someone who is so dear to me like you! One of the reasons that I can write so freely is because I know you are out there, and that you've got my back, in your infinite wisdom, and you won't let me down. Thank you for your time, talent, love and support. Xoxoxo

To my food photographer, Denise Chastain, who went above and beyond so many times, in so many ways, thank you doesn't even begin to cut it. Your participation in this project took this book to a whole other level. When we first started working together, you hardly knew me, but that did not stop you from giving 150 percent of yourself to our shoots because that is who you are, and it shows! I feel so honored and grateful to have been able to work with you, and learn from you. I am in awe of your amazing talent and your incredible energy; you are a total dynamo, and I am the luckiest cookbook author in the world!!!!!!

And last, but absolutely not least, to my dear Christen Napier, who literally put this book together for me, and helped me lay out, and design, everything that you see before you; I must have done something really great in a past life to deserve such an amazing friend and work partner as you. I consider this book to be just as much yours as mine. You have been there, by my side, through every twist and turn in the road, through every photo shoot, mishap, and event involving this book. You are my rock, and I don't know what I would have done without you. I love working with you, I love laughing with you, and I love you! and I told you, I am taking you on a cruise around the world and I mean it!!!!!!!! Thank you, thank you, thank you.

Until he extends the circle of his
compassion to all living things,
man will not himself find peace.

- Albert Schweitzer

Introduction

Why do people continue to eat meat in America in the 20th century despite the rising health concerns, immoral treatment of factory farmed animals, and the disastrous effects of factory farming on our environment?

I will give you one absolute answer: because, to most people, meat tastes good. If it tasted bad no one would eat it. Not even the people who think that they need meat to feel good, or that God put those animals here for us to eat, or that we are at the "top" of the food chain, and other animals eat other animals, so why shouldn't we? Even these people would not eat meat if it tasted disgusting.

So really, it all boils down to these tiny little bumps on our tongues that we call taste-buds. It is amazing that such a tiny part of our anatomy can have such an enormous influence on our habits, actions, and behavior.

I understand. When I was little, I would tell people with great enthusiasm, "I am a meat and potatoes girl!" I hated having to eat my salad at dinnertime, but boy was I in heaven when I had my meatloaf and mashed potatoes.

I was also born loving animals. I spent whole days catching frogs in ponds so I could touch them and play with them. I read "Ranger Rick" magazines, and dreamed of becoming a naturalist. I worried about stray dogs and injured birds. I convinced my parents to let me have fish, hermit crabs, hamsters, racoons, bunnies, a guinea pig, a parrot, cats, and a horse.

Then one day at dinner I made a stunning connection. I was eating an animal! Strange that it was possible to remain detached from this fact for so long without it ever having registered on a deeper level. I guess there is a first time for everything. This realization forever changed my life. It was the beginning of a lifelong path for me. A journey that started by not eating meat, but eating fish, back once briefly to eating meat, all the way up to today where I am fully vegetarian, and eat no animal products at all (except when I was working on certain sections of this book.)

Just like my story, this book is designed to take you on a journey. An adventure into a new and delicious land. Remember those little taste buds I was talking about? Well, the best thing about them is that they can be fooled! I am now a "veggie-meat" and potatoes girl, and my taste buds don't know the difference! By eating immitation meat dishes, I can have the TASTE of meat anytime I want, without ever participating in the destruction of another living being.

I want you to experience how incredible veggie-meat dishes can taste as well, and that is what this book is all about. No recipe makes it into this cookbook unless it has successfully "fooled" and/or fully satisfied a true meat enthusiast. In fact, most of my taste-testers tell me that not only do my dishes taste like the real thing, but they taste BETTER than the real thing!

We are a nation of animal lovers. Most people who have pets consider them to be a member of their family. If someone spoke up in a lecture hall and said "raise your hand if you are against cruelty to animals," I cannot imagine anyone who would not raise their hand. And yet, most of those same people would happily go out for dinner afterwards and order a hamburger, completely without thinking, just like I did.

Most people are completely disconnected from what they are eating, and those who are not, are unaware, or in denial, about the brutal and inhumane treatment that factory farm animals are subjected to, and their own personal involvement in that process. I want people to realize that by buying and consuming meat, and other animal products, they are directly supporting and perpetuating the WORST kind of cruelty to animals. Cruelty that is driven by cutting corners to facilitate consumer demand. And that consumer is YOU! As a consumer you have enormous power. You, along with other like-minded individuals, have the power to turn an industry upside-down by refusing to buy it's products. A business can only exist as long as it has customers.

The ancient phillosopher Plutarch said, "But for the sake of some little mouthfull of flesh, we deprive a soul of the sun and light and of that proportion of life and time that it had been born into the world to enjoy."

27 million farm animals are killed in the United States alone each day.

If animals could speak our language they would say, "Don't Eat Me!"

This book is dedicated to them.

About the Woodstock Farm Animal Sanctuary and Its Animal Ambassadors

All of the farm animals featured in this book are residents of The Woodstock Farm Animal Sanctuary in Woodstock, NY, to which a percentage of the profits of this book are donated. WFAS is a safe haven for farm animals who have been rescued from abuse and neglect. The sanctuary provides these animals with a caring home where they can live out their lives in peace.

WFAS was founded in 2004 by Jenny Brown and Doug Abel, whose simple philosophy is that "kindness and respect to animals is our moral duty, and that all the creatures that share this earth are here with us and not for us."

WFAS is such an outstanding and special place that it has won "Non-Profit of the Year" in the prestigious Veggie Awards held by Veg News magazine. WFAS's goal is to educate the public about the inhumane treatment of factory farmed animals, and to spread awareness about alternatives to a meat-eating and animal-product-consuming lifestyle.

It is the animals themselves that really bring this message home.

I would like to introduce you to the animal ambassadors featured in this book. All have their own stories, and all represent a lucky few that have escaped the terrible fate of an animal raised in intensive confinement, darkness, and misery on America's factory farms.

First up is Sheila; our beautiful poster-girl for the Chicken Free chapter:

Sheila was no more than a "spring-chicken" when I snapped the shot of her galavanting on the lawn at WFAS a couple years back. She was born in an elementary school as part of a classroom hatching project. One of the teachers at the school notified WFAS when she discovered that the chicks were becoming sickly due to improper care. Sheila was taken to WFAS, and the teachers were sent information on humane alternatives to live animal projects. Beautiful Sheila had a short but happy life at the farm sanctuary. "Broiler" hens like Sheila are bred to grow to slaughter weight in 45 days. Their organs and skeletons cannot keep up with this unnaturally escalated rate of growth, and so most of them have weak hearts. Although chickens can live up to 15 years, Sheila died of a heart attack when she was less than two years old.

Sheila led a charmed life in comparison to the billions of other "broiler" chickens who suffer on America's factory farms. These birds live in atrociously overcrowded sheds with thousands upon thousands of other birds. Many are too weak to fight for access to food and water, and many others are trampled, and suffocated underneath the other birds. Chickens raised like this for human consumption almost never see sunlight, and the air they breathe is putrid with the poisonous waste gasses of methane and ammonia. After seven weeks of suffering under these conditions they are sent to slaughter.

Next is Dylan; our darling cow representative for the Cow-Free section, and also featured when he was a baby in the Dairy & Egg Free chapter:

Little Dylan was found tied to a post, and stuck to the ground in his own feces at a dairy farm in upstate New York. A compassionate couple who were driving by saw the little calf in this horrible condition and convinced the farmer to give him to them. Like most dairy calves, he had been taken away from his mother within hours/days of being born, and was soon to be sent to slaughter and turned into veal. The couple brought him to WFAS.

Dylan was 1 week old when he arrived at WFAS in August of 2005. Weak and traumatized, it took him a little while to realize he was safe, but he soon became the darling of the farm. On his first birthday he had gained 800 pounds, and was treated to a homemade birthday "cake" made of fruit in a bread shell with a carrot candle. Dylan is now all grown up and towers over everybody there, but he still loves hugs and kisses as much as when he first arrived at the farm. To see pictures of Dylan's first birthday party you can go to WFAS's website which is WoodstockFAS.org.

Then we have Pinky and Eva; our playful piglet ambassadors for the Pig Free chapter:

Being in a pen full of piglets is like being in a pen full of puppies; they could not be more excited and happy to meet you. The first time I tried to take their picture, it was from a seated position n a haybale inside their pen. Both Pinky and Eva, and their two siblings, Wally and Nemo, pictured in the back of the book, all jumped on me at the same time! I had to wait until they calmed down so they would hold still long enough for me to take their picture!

These adorable little guys were born on a freezing cold New Years Eve along with 10 other piglets. The farmer had just purchased the mother sow to butcher for meat and had no idea that she was pregnant. Eight of the other piglets froze to death as the mother sow had no warm place to give birth. Pinky and Eva, along with Wally and Nemo, were rushed to a local wildlife rehabilitator, who fell in love with the piglets, and refused to give them back. She brought them to WFAS to save them from being raised and slaughtered for meat.

Here's to you kind lady, and to my little piglet friends! Long may you live in peace!

Meet Celia; our sweetheart sheep friend who posed so gracefully in non-wool scarves for our Holidays chapter:

Celia spent the first 4 years of her life on a farm that raised sheep for wool. The farm was going out of business, and the farmer was nice enough to give Celia and some other sheep to a farm animal sanctuary in Pennsylvania, instead of sending them to slaughter, which would normally be the case. After 8 years in Pennsylvania, Celia came to live at WFAS.

The day that I took this picture of Celia, she had been separated from the other sheep because she was not feeling well, and had not been eating. Everyone at the farm said that our little photo-shoot definitely cheered her up. She seemed to feel very special with her scarves on, and with all the attention that she was getting. After our photo-shoot she ate a whole tray of wheatgrass!

Celia passed on from liver failure a month after these pictures were taken. Thank you Celia, for being so patient and accomodating while I took your picture. I will miss seeing you, and looking into your gentle eyes the next time I visit the farm.

We have more animal ambassadors in the Kid's Menu chapter of the book, including Snowball the goat, Isabella the chicken, and Alfonso the turkey. To learn more about them and the Woodstock Farm Animal Sanctuary, you can visit them on the web at WoodstockFAS.org.

You can also visit WFAS in person, and meet and mingle with the animals yourselves. WFAS is approximately 2 hours north of NYC, and is open to the public on weekends from April through October.

A MESSAGE FROM THE WOODSTOCK FARM ANIMAL SANCTUARY:
The Woodstock Farm Animal Sanctuary wishes to thank the author for including our organization in the pages of this book, and for a portion of the proceeds of the sales. We would like to express that a vegetarian diet is most certainly a giant step in the right direction, but a vegan diet, completely void of animal products, is the most compassionate, environmentally-friendly, and healthy diet one can have.

Guidelines For Best Results

There are many brands of veggie-meat available today in the marketplace. Some are better than others, and all are surpisingly different in taste, ingredients, and texture. For each recipe, I recommend a specific brand of veggie-meat and/or meat-flavored broth that I think tastes the best for that recipe in particular. I have nothing against adventurous experimentation, and you might even stumble onto a delicious find on your own, but I cannot guarantee the same great results that I achieve if you decide to use a different brand from the one that I recommend.

All of the brands that I recommend can be found at most major supermarkets and/or health food stores, with the exception of the veggie-turkey in the holiday section. This veggie-meat can only be found at an authentic Asian market. If you are having trouble locating a brand of veggie-meat, ask your local supermarket manager to order it for you. Usually they are more than happy to do so.

Most veggie-meats contain some form of soy ingredient. For consumers who are allergic to soy, or wish to avoid it, there is a fantastic brand of veggie-meat called Quorn which I recommend frequently throughout this book. Quorn veggie-meat is soy free, and is, in my opinion, one of the best brands out there.

What Do Vegetarians Eat?

O.k. So you love my recipes, and you really could eat them day and night because they are so unbelievably delicious. As understandable as that is, one cannot live on veggie-meat alone! A healthy vegetarian diet includes lots of other foods, and NO diet is complete without many daily servings of fresh fruits and vegetables. The name of the game is balance, my friends. So, here is a list of great vegetarian foods that you can enjoy when you are not eating my dishes:

*pesto pasta, tomato bruschetta, stuffed shells, eggplant parmesan, eggplant rollatini, vegetable lasagna, ratatouille, pasta with garlic and broccoli, macaroni and cheese, pasta with marinara sauce, baked ziti, pasta primavera (pasta with vegetables), pizza, garlic knots, zeppoli, garlic bread, granola bars, oatmeal, grits, cream of wheat, fruit smoothies, yogurt, breakfast cereals, almond butter and jelly, sunflower butter and banana, almonds, walnuts, cashews, pecans, hummus, garlic hummus, olive hummus, falafels, chick peas, rice and black beans, rice and pinto beans, bean burrito, bean and rice burrito, guacamole and chips, tomato salsa and chips, mango salsa and chips, vegetable fajitas, fried plantains, jalapeno poppers, cheese quesadillas, fried zucchini sticks, beer battered mushrooms, ice-pops, sherbert, bagels and cream cheese, bagels and vegetable cream cheese, french onion dip, spinach dip, spinach and artichoke dip, vegetable quiche, risotto with wild mushrooms, vegetable fried rice, vegetable spring rolls, vegetable dumplings, moo shoo vegetable, broccoli with garlic sauce, string beans with black bean sauce, sesame tofu, vegetable stir-fry with brown rice, vegetable lo mein, cold sesame noodles, brussel sprouts, broccoli rabe, kale, corn on the cob, sweet potatoes, sweet potato fries, french fries, onion rings, potato pancakes, applesauce, pretzels, potato chips, popcorn, cornbread, blueberry muffins, banana bread, fruit salad, vegetarian stuffed mushrooms, artichokes hollandaise, artichokes vinagrette, tabouli, vegetable tempura, avocado rolls, cucumber rolls, asparagus rolls, spinach salad, arugala and beet salad, tomato and cucumber salad, pickles, coleslaw, potato salad, field green salad with balsamic vinaigrette, pears, watermelon, pineapple, papaya, strawberries, strawberries dipped in chocolate, dried apricots, figs, prunes, mushroom pate, cheese fondue, vegetarian soups: (check that they are made with vegetable broth and contain no meat shreds) miso soup, butternut squash soup, black bean soup, minestrone, pasta fagioli, potato soup, cream of mushroom, cream of broccoli, tomato soup, tomato and rice soup, lentil soup, carrot soup, corn chowder, vegetable barley soup, pea soup, mushroom barley soup, cauliflower soup, potato leek soup, peanut soup, gazpacho, cold avocado soup, cold melon soup, cold cucumber soup, baked potato with broccoli and cheddar, baked potato with sour cream and chives, baked potato, hash browns, mashed potatoes, biscuits, english muffins, scones, scrambled eggs, vegetable omelets, vegetable frittata, egg-salad sandwiches, grilled cheese sandwiches, fried green tomatoes, hush puppies, potato pierogies, potato and onion pierogies, gnocchi, zucchini bread, brownies, chocolate chip cookies, apple crisp, apple pie, blueberry pie, cherry pie, pecan pie, pumpkin pie, Baba Ghannouj (baked eggplant dip), Dal (Indian split pea dish), vegetable curry, Baingan Bhartha (eggplant curry), Indian vegetable Samosas, Raita (Indian yogurt sauce), Palak Paneer (spinach and cheese dish) Naan (Indian bread), Greek salad, stuffed grape leaves, couscous, spanikopita (greek phyllo dough with spinach and feta), pancakes, waffles, french toast, chocolate crepes, chocolate croissants ....
and a zillion other things!*

A Word About Cheese

Not all cheese is vegetarian. Most people are shocked to learn this and I was no exception. I had been a vegetarian for most of my life before I was made aware of this fact, and had been unknowingly and happily consuming every kind of cheese for years, considering it to be one of the staples of my vegetarian lifestyle.

The truth is, most European hard cheeses such as cheddar, mozzarella and Parmesan are produced using animal rennet, which is an enzyme that is usually obtained from the stomach lining of freshly slaughtered calves. Rennet is an enzyme that stimulates milk to harden into cheese curds. The curds are then separated from the liquid (whey) which then mature into various types of cheeses.

Soft cheeses such as cream cheese are vegetarian because they are acid-set, which means they are produced by adding bacterial cultures to milk instead of rennet.

Other animal-derived enzymes used in the making of cheese are lipase and pepsin. Lipase comes from the tongues of slaughtered baby goats, goats, calves and lambs. Lipase is used to give certain cheeses stronger flavor by speeding up the breakdown of milk-fat. Pepsin is obtained from the stomach of pigs and is sometimes used in conjunction with rennet in the cheese-making process. Rennet, lipase and pepsin are often simply listed on cheese labels as "enzymes."

So does all this mean that as a dedicated vegetarian you can never eat many of your favorite cheeses again?

Not by a long shot!

Today, more and more cheeses are being made with microbial or vegetable rennets. Microbial rennet can be obtained from certain microorganisms through a process of fermentation, or it can be genetically manufactured. Genetically manufactured microbial rennet contains a synthesized version of the active ingredient in animal rennet (chymosin). Both types of microbial rennet are suitable for vegetarians.

Vegetable-derived rennets come from plant sources such as fig leaves, melon, wild thistle and safflower.

Trader Joe's has an amazing variety of vegetarian cheeses that represent almost every main kind of cheese you can think of. They are all very clearly labeled as containing vegetable or microbial rennets. Trader Joe's even has a "Rennet List" on their web site, which lists a sample of their cheeses and the rennet-source that they contain. Whole Foods carries vegetarian cheese and is also very conscientious about clearly labeling the ingredients in their products.

Many kosher cheeses are vegetarian and can be found in most major supermarkets. Look for kosher cheese that clearly states that it is 100% vegetarian and contains no animal rennet. "Veggie Slices," which can be found in the produce section of markets like A&P and Stop and Shop, contain no animal rennet, and have become a very popular vegetarian cheese option for many shoppers.

Every kind of cheese that is listed in the recipes of this book is available in vegetarian form from one of the sources listed above

What About Fish?

Vegetarians do not eat fish. Fish are sentient beings, just like cows, dogs, cats, and other animals, including humans. They have a subjective awareness of their own experiences and surroundings, and they feel pleasure as well as pain. I do not have a fish-free chapter in this book because I am not aware of any popular brands of veggie-fish available in any major supermarkets. This does not mean that I have forgotten about the fishies!!

Many people are skeptical about fish experiencing pain despite the numerous scientific studies that prove that they do. The fact is, fish not only experience physical pain, but psychological pain as well. I stopped eating fish when I learned that many farmed fish actually go insane from being kept in bathtubs with so many other fish that they can only swim in place day after day. They often begin banging their heads against the sides of the tub, much as a severely distraught human would bang their head against a wall.

Choosing not to eat fish, as well as other animals, is a great way to participate in conscious non-violence towards other living beings, and the earth itself. Commercial fishing is the number one cause of the ever-increasing destruction of the earth's oceans. We have already over-fished so many parts of the world's oceans that we have un-balanced entire ecosystems. Places that were once brimming with life, are now under-water ghost-towns.

As Marvin Gaye sings in his song "Mercy, Mercy Me", when he is talking about the earth being pillaged by humans, he says, "How much more abuse from man can she stand?" Good question, Marvin. Not much more.

Sheila

Chicken-Free

*To become a vegetarian is to step into
the stream that leads to nirvana.*
- Buddha

Chicken-Free Noodle Soup
Chicken-Free Thai Style Noodle Soup
Let's Go Crazy Chicken-Free Potato Croquettes

Popeye's Chicken-Free Salad
Pasta with Chickpea Pesto
Chicken-Free Asparagus Sushi Rolls

Cool as a Cucumber Chicken-Free Hummus Wraps
Over the Rainbow Chicken-Free Pita with Mango Raita
Cuckoo for Coconut No-Chicken
Pasta Robino
From Russia with Love
No-Chicken at the Ritz

Chicken-Free Noodle Soup

Even the toughest guy turns into a Cindy-Lou-Who when they get sick. And what do they want? They want mommy and her chicken noodle soup. Well, I have to tell you, this recipe can't replace dear old mom, but it will knock the socks off of her soup and give her a darn good run for her money. Guaranteed to comfort, soothe and taste delicious anytime. Serves 6

-1 large onion, chopped
-2 leeks (white part only) cleaned well and chopped
-3 garlic cloves, minced
-15-20 baby carrots, chopped
-1 celery stalk, chopped
-1 large potato, peeled and diced
-3 cubes chicken FLAVORED stock (recommend America's Choice) OR 2 boxes G. Washington's Golden
 Seasoning and Broth (you will be using 9 of the .13 oz. packets mixed with 2 quarts of water)
-1 tbsp. dried parsley flakes
-5 shakes black pepper
-1/2 lb gemelli pasta or pasta of choice
-1 10 oz. box no-chicken strips or no-chicken cut into strips (recommend Quorn brand)
-2 tbsp. olive oil
-3 1/2 cups of water
* For a lower-sodium soup use 2 quarts of vegetable broth

1. Put all vegetables in a large soup pot. Add America's Choice stock cubes or G. Washington's broth packets to 2 quarts of water, and bring to a boil, stirring until boullion is dissolved completely. Add spices, reduce heat and simmer for one hour, stirring occasionally.
2. Meanwhile start water boiling in separate pot for pasta.
3. In medium skillet cook no-chicken strips in olive oil according to instructions. Remove from heat and drain on paper towels to remove excess oil. Chop into medium size pieces and set aside.
4. Cook pasta. Drain and rinse with cold water. Set aside.
5. Scoop 2 cups of solid ingredients out of broth. Blend in a blender until smooth add back to the pot. Add no-chicken, pasta and 3 1/2 cups of water. Stir and heat on medium low for several minutes.
6. Ladle into bowls. Now THIS is some "chicken" noodle soup for your soul.

Chicken-Free Thai-Style Noodle Soup

I can't say enough about how swooningly good this is. It simply takes you away. I took some basic ingredients used in Thai cooking and threw them all together to make a delicious soup without nearly as daunting a list of the ingredients that usually accompany most Asian recipes. It is remarkably simple to make, exotically fantastic to eat, and it will take you to beautiful places where nothing matters; nothing at all. Serves 6

-2 tbsp. vegetable oil
-3 cloves garlic, diced
-1 tbsp. fresh ginger root, peeled and diced
-1 medium shallot, diced
-6 c. clear vegetable broth
-1 14 oz. can coconut milk
-2 oz. packet or 2 tablespoons red curry paste (places like Whole foods and Super Stop and Shop have it, as well as Asian markets)
-juice of 1 lime
-1/4 c. apple juice
-10 oz. no-chicken (recommend Quorn naked cutlets)
-9 oz. ramen noodles or 3 packages ramen noodles.
- chopped cilantro for garnish (optional)

1. Heat oil in a wok or large pot. Sauté garlic, ginger and shallots over medium heat 3-4 minutes. Add vegetable broth, coconut milk and curry paste. Stir and bring to a boil. Reduce to a simmer. Add lime and apple juice.
2. Cook no-chicken and ramen noodles separately according to instructions. Keep separate from broth.
3. To serve: heap noodles into a bowl and add plenty of chopped chunks of no-chicken. Stir broth well before ladling plenty on top. Garnish with cilantro if you wish. La-La-Land, here you come!

Let's Go Crazy Chicken-Free Potato Croquettes

Insanely yummy!!!! Perfectly crisp on the outside and deliciously tasty on the inside with tons of fabulous fried flavor that is incredibly light. It's hard to remain calm when you are eating something so spectacular, so why even bother trying? Go crazy! Makes 20-25 croquettes

-5 large yukon gold potatoes, peeled and chopped
-2 tbsp. butter
-10 oz. can condensed cream of mushroom soup
-1/2 c. milk
-2 tsp. dried parsley flakes
-1 tsp. salt
-5 shakes black pepper
-20 oz. no-chicken strips (recommend Quorn brand)
-1/2 c. flour
-2 eggs, beaten with 2 tbsp. cold water
-9 oz. bag panko breadcrumbs
-48 oz. vegetable oil

1. Boil potatoes in lightly salted water until super soft. Drain, and in a large bowl, mash in butter, mushroom soup, milk, parsley, salt and pepper until nice and smooth.
2. Cook no-chicken according to instructions. Chop into medium sized chunks and mix evenly into potato mixture. Refrigerate for 2 hours (in a crunch? Put in freezer for 45 minutes).
3. Form potato-mix into fat sausage-like croquettes. Roll each one in flour, dip in eggs and then coat with a generous amount of breadcrumbs.
4. Deep fry in small batches until golden brown. Remove with large slotted spoon and drain on paper towels. Let cool for 5 minutes. Serve with broiled tomatoes, salad and bread. A really extravagant treat!

Popeye's Chicken-Free Salad Sandwich

I know Popeye is not a real person, but he would love this spinach-packed delicious treat of a chicken-free salad sandwich. It will help you grow up big and strong no matter what age you are. You don't want to be wimpy like that Wimpy who eats hamburgers all day! No, no. It's easy and delicious, so flex your muscles and let's get started. Serves 2

-10 oz. no-chicken (recommend Quorn naked cutlets)
-1/2 c. of your favorite store bought spinach dip
-fresh, organic baby spinach

1. Cook no-chicken according to instructions, and cut into medium-sized chunks. Stick in fridge for about ten minutes until cool not cold.
2. In a medium bowl mix no-chicken with spinach dip. Serve at room temperature with fresh baby spinach on sourdough or country bread. Can-crushingly good!

"If a man aspires towards a righteous life, his first act of abstinence is from injury to animals." - Albert Einstein

Pasta with Chickpea Pesto

The consistency of this pasta sauce is like velvet on your tongue. Chick peas are substituted for the traditional pine nuts that are used in pesto to make it super soft, and the sundried tomatoes are thrown in just to tickle your tastebuds. Can easily go undercover as a pasta salad for picnics and pot-luck suppers. Delicious and nutritious! Serves 6-8

-2 9.5 oz. boxes frozen, unbreaded no-chicken patties (recommend Morning Star Farms Grillers Chik'n)
-1 c. sundried tomatoes, sliced in small strips
-2 tbsp. olive oil
-2 lightly packed cups basil leaves, cleaned
-2 cloves garlic
-2 tsp. dried parsley flakes
-1 c. olive oil
-1 15 oz. can chick-peas (garbanzo beans), drained
-3-4 shakes salt
-4 shakes black pepper
-1 lb rotini, fusili or penne pasta

1. Cook no-chicken patties for 3 minutes on each side (or per instructions) in 2 tbsp. oil in non-stick skillet with sundried tomatoes. Be careful not to blacken the sundrieds.
2. Put basil, garlic, parsley flakes, olive oil and 3/4 of a cup of chick-peas (reserve the rest for later) into a blender and pulse until well-mixed and fairly smooth. Transfer to a small saucepan and heat, stirring for several minutes until warm. Add 3-4 shakes each of salt and pepper and mix well. Remove from heat.
3. Cook pasta according to instructions in lightly salted water. Drain and mix with all other ingredients adding the remainder of whole chickpeas to the mix. Stir, and let sit 10-15 minutes until about room temperature.

Chicken-Free Asparagus Sushi Rolls

Sushi? Yes sushi. Sushi does not have to be raw and it does not have to contain fish! This sushi tastes just as delectable as any California or shrimp roll, and you get to have the fun of rolling it yourself. Rolling your own sushi has become a popular party theme. Try other fillings such as sliced avocado, baked tofu, shredded carrots or whatever else you might like. The only "special" tools you need are a super sharp knife and an appetite for lots of sushi!! Makes 50-60 pieces

-1 c. uncooked short grain sushi rice (can be found in Asian section of most major supermarkets. Most brands will specify that the rice is for sushi. Avoid using regular rice)
-1/3 c. rice vinegar
-10-12 oz no-chicken (recommend Quorn brand)
-1 bundle thin asparagus spears
-2 tsp. wasabi powder (can be found in Asian section of supermarket) *
-1/4 c. mayonnaise *
-1 box nori sheets (The toasted seaweed sheets that sushi is wrapped in. Can also be found in Asian section)
* If you can find wasabi mayonnaise that is already prepared, by all means just buy that instead of the mayo and wasabi powder
Soy sauce

1. Cook rice according to instructions. As soon as the rice is done, add rice vinegar and mix and fluff with fork. Set aside to cool.
2. Meanwhile cook no-chicken according to instructions. Slice into medium- thin, short strips and set aside to cool.
3. Cut tips off asparagus leaving about 1/4 of the stem attached. Steam over boiling water for two minutes until bright green and crunchy. Cut in half or in thirds.
4. Mix 1 tsp. wasabi powder with one tsp. water until it forms a greenish paste. Let sit, covered, ten minutes. This will be your "glue" for sealing the edges of Nori to make the ends stick together when you roll it up.
5. Mix remaining 1 tsp. wasabi the same way with one tsp. water. Let sit ten minutes and add mayo. Mix until you have wasabi mayonaise!

6. Now you are ready to Roll!!!! Cut nori sheets in half lengthwise. Lay nori sheet shiny side DOWN on a cutting board or flat surface. You will need a bowl of water to dip your fingers in because the rice is very sticky. Dip fingers in water and pick up a small amount of rice and spread it thinly and evenly across the nori leaving 1 inch with no rice at the end. (On the long side, NOT the wide side) In the exact center of the rice spread a thin line of wasabi mayonaise from one end to the next. On this line, arrange a piece of no chicken and a piece of asparagus right next to each other. Continue on down the line. With your finger, spread the plain wasabi paste on the inch of nori with no rice. Roll the nori over carefully and slowly trying to put even pressure on both ends. Squeeze a little as you go so the filling doesn't flop out. Bring edges together and seal by pressing down on the two edges for several seconds. I will tell you right away that your first one will probably be a disaster but it will still taste great anyway. By the third one you should have it down! Cut your roll in sections (6 or 8 per roll) using your very sharp knife, dipping the knife in water and wiping it clean between cuts. Serve at room temperature or chilled. Dip sushi in soy sauce or whatever accompaniment you enjoy. After your first batch, you will feel like a pro!

QUICK TIP: Cooking sushi rice can be kind of an involved process. I recommend just ordering some already cooked from a Japanese restaurant. In this case, ask for a quart of sushi rice.

Cool as a Cucumber Chicken-Free Hummus Wraps

These are easy, delicious and so refreshing, and perfect for ladies who lunch on a hot summer day. (Gentlemen will enjoy them equally.) Serves 4

-6 frozen, unbreaded no-chicken patties (recommend Morning Star Farms Grillers Chik'n)
-4 tsp. olive oil
-1/8 tsp. paprika
-pinch of cumin
-6 tbsp. garlic hummus
-4 large sundried tomato or spinach wraps
-small cucumber, peeled and cut in thin slices
-1 c. pitted kalamata olives, sliced

1. Cook no-chicken in olive oil in non-stick skillet for as long as package suggests. Sprinkle with paprika and cumin while cooking. Transfer to a plate and cut into thin slices. Put in freezer to cool down for ten minutes.
2. Spread a thin layer of hummus over most of the surface of each wrap (about 1 1/2 tbsp. per wrap). Divide no-chicken, cucumbers, and olives into 4 equal portions and spread each portion on the hummus-covered surface of a wrap. Wrap snugly, cut in half, or in fifths, skewer with fancy toothpicks, and gossip away.

"The question is not, Can they REASON? Nor can they TALK?
But, Can they SUFFER?" - Jeremy Bentham, An Introduction to
the Principles of Morals & Legislation

Over the Rainbow Chicken-Free Pita with Mango Raita

This dish is a tune for your taste-buds to sing out loud. Your troubles will melt like lemon drops! You'll be way above the chimney tops! Fresh mango, Indian spices, warm, toasty pita bread, juicy no-chicken and spinach. It's almost too good to be true, but it is! So sing it baby! Serves 4-6

-4 tbsp. olive oil
-1/2 c. finely diced onion
-1 tsp. diced fresh ginger
-1 tsp. salt
-3 shakes black pepper
-1/2 tsp. sugar
-20 oz. spinach, washed, de-stemmed and chopped
-1/3 c. water
-14 oz. no-chicken (recommend Quorn naked cutlets)
-1 pinch each of ground cinnamon, nutmeg, cumin and cayenne pepper
-6 whole wheat pita pockets

MANGO RAITA:
-1 c. plain yogurt
-pinch ground nutmeg
-1 tbsp. honey
-1 mango, chopped into small chunks
-2 tbsp. slivered toasted almonds

QUICK TIP: Buy 10 oz. chopped frozen sprinach. Defrost and drain out excess water before cooking.

1. Heat olive oil in large pot. Add onions and saute for about three minutes. Next add ginger, salt, black pepper, and sugar. Add spinach a little bit at a time until it is all completely wilted. Add water and bring to a simmer. Reduce heat to low, cover and cook for ten minutes.

2. Meanwhile cook no-chicken according to instructions and chop into medium sized chunks.

3. Mix all ingredients for mango raita in a medium bowl and set aside.

4. When ten minutes is up on your spinach, add no-chicken, cinnamon, nutmeg, cumin, and cayenne pepper. Stir and cook for a couple minutes on medium -low to let flavors blend.

5. Lightly toast pita-pockets and cut in half. Using a slotted spoon to drain off excess liquid, fill pocket with spinach/no-chick mix. Spoon raita on top of each pocket and serve. Blue-birds fly!

Cuckoo for Coconut No-Chicken

This is a massive party favorite. Anyone who is a fan of coconut will go completely bonkers for this coconut no-chicken with a sweet hint of mango in the background. There are just no words. Makes about 30 pieces

-1 c. flour
-1 tsp. salt
-1 tsp. baking powder
-1/4 tsp. turmeric
-1/4 tsp. cayenne pepper
-pinch allspice
-3/4 c. mango nectar (juice)
-1 c. canned coconut milk
-20 oz. no-chicken, thawed, and cut into no-chicken nugget sized chunks (recommend Quorn naked cutlets)
- 48 oz. corn oil
-2/3 of 14 oz. bag sweetened, dried coconut flakes (baking section of supermarket)
- 1 c. plain breadcrumbs

1. Whisk flour, salt, baking powder, turmeric, cayenne pepper and allspice in a large bowl and then whisk in the mango nectar and coconut milk. Add no-chicken and stir gently to fully coat in batter. Leave to sit at room temp. for about 30 minutes.
2. Heat oil in a wok or large pot using a deep-frying/candy thermometer to determine when the oil reaches 350.
3. In a large bowl thoroughly mix breadcrumbs and coconut flakes. Press and coat pieces of no-chicken into this mixture until completely covered. Gently shake-off any really loose bits. Drop gently into oil, frying no more than 5 or 6 at a time. Cook about 30 seconds to 1 minute until golden brown. Remove with slotted spoon or tongs and drain on paper towels. Serve as is or with an accompanying sauce such as a mango salsa.

Pasta Robino

This pasta has a superb zing to it along with a juicy juiciness that you will fall in love with. It is based on an Italian dish that traditionaly uses anchovies (yucky, yucky, blach)! I use delicious no-chicken and delectable kalamata olives instead. Serves 4

-3 tbsp. olive oil
-4 cloves garlic, diced
-2 hot cherry peppers, seeded and diced fine (can be found in a jar near the pickle section)
-1 tsp. parsley flakes
-1 28 oz. can whole peeled plum tomatoes
-1/4 c. capers, drained
-1/2 c. pitted kalamata olives, drained and chopped
-4 shakes black pepper
-1/8 tsp. salt
-1/4 tsp. oregano
-9.5 oz. frozen, unbreaded no-chicken patties (recommend Morning Star Farms Grillers Chik'n)
-1 lb spaghetti, fusilli, or rotini pasta
-parmesan cheese (optional)

1. Heat oil over medium heat. Sauté garlic, hot cherry peppers and parsley for several minutes. Add tomatoes and bring to a simmer. Mash tomatoes until the sauce is not too chunky. Stir in capers, olives, black pepper, salt and oregano. Simmer for 10-12 minutes and then reduce heat to low.
2. Meanwhile, cook no-chicken according to instructions and then slice into bite size pieces.
3. Cook pasta in salted water, drain, and toss with sauce and no-chicken. Serve with parmesan cheese if you so desire.

"Live simply, so that others may simply live." - Gandhi

From Russia with Love

This meal makes a perfect romantic dinner for two comrades. It was inspired by a Russian dish called Chicken Kiev that I used to love as a kid before I knew where chicken came from. Now I would much rather eat this delicious easy to make no-chicken dinner. It's got a lot more love in it. Serves 2

-1 c. rice
-small loaf stale crusty bread OR 1/4 cup plain breadcrumbs
-10 oz. no-chicken (recommend Quorn or Lightlife)
-1/4 c. butter
-3 cloves garlic, diced fine
-1 tbsp. lemon juice
-1 tsp. parsley flakes
-1 tsp. dried chives
-1/2 tsp. dried tarragon leaves
-1/2 tsp. ground mustard
-1/8 tsp. cayenne pepper
-1/4 tsp. salt
-4 shakes black pepper

1. Cook rice according to instructions and set aside.
2. Preheat oven to 375°. Grate stale bread with cheese grater until you have 1/4 cup breadcrumbs. Spread out on baking sheet and toast until brown, 8-10 minutes. Remove from oven and set aside.
3. Defrost no-chicken. Cut into bite-sized pieces. Meanwhile melt 1/4 cup butter in medium skillet. Add garlic and sauté several minutes over medium heat. Next stir in lemon juice and all of the spices. Add no-chicken and cook for 4-6 minutes in melted garlic-herb butter.
4. Serve hot over rice with breadcrumbs sprinkled lightly on top. Yummy, yummy, love in the tummy.

No-Chicken at The Ritz

This dish is quite a dish. Superb and oh so very gourmet. The kind of entree you would expect to find at only the finest establishments. So if you want to impress someone, or just impress yourself, this dinner is the ticket. Serves 4

-2 tbsp. butter
-1 lb no-chicken (recommend Quorn brand)
-1 14 oz. can artichoke hearts (in WATER), chopped
-3-4 shakes salt
-3-4 shakes black pepper
-1/4 c. white wine
-1/3 c. vegetable broth
-1 tsp. flour
-1 lb polenta (already cooked. Comes in a roll often
 located near nasty hot dogs. You can also make the
 polenta from scratch, spread out in a single layer and
 refrigerate for at least 3 hours until firm)
-olive oil
-6 oz goat cheese
-1/2 c. chopped pitted prunes

1. Melt butter over medium heat and cook no-chicken several minutes. Add artichoke, salt and pepper, stir and let them settle in together for a minute or so. Add wine, veggie broth and whisk in flour. Bring to a simmer, turn off and set aside.
2. Slice polenta about a quarter- inch thick and cut into triangles. Arrange on lightly oiled broiling pan. Brush tops of triangles lightly with olive oil. Broil on low until the tops begin to turn golden brown. Remove from oven and top each triangle with a medium smear of goat cheese and broil several more minutes until goat cheese is warm and relaxed looking.
3. Arrange plate with polenta triangles as the bed and ladle the no-chicken mix on top. Sprinkle a palm-full of chopped prunes over each portion and Voila!! Don't forget to put your napkin in your lap!!!

Dylan

Cow-Free

I have no doubt that it is a part of the destiny of the human race, in it's gradual improvement, to leave off eating animals.
- Henry David Thoreau

Szechuan-Style Soup with No-Beef
Potluck No-Meatball Samosas

Amazing No-Meatballs
Johnny's Tofu No-Meatballs
Magnificent Manicotti with Red Pepper Cream Sauce
Big Guy Stuffed Peppers

Righteous Reuben Sandwiches
Football Sunday Philly Cheese No-Steaks
Beef StrogaNOT
No-Steak Houdini
Mini Mandarin Orange Jello-Shot Cupcakes

Szechuan-Style Soup with No-Beef

This wonderfully warming soup was inspired by a popular Chinese dish called Szechuan beef. Instead of the traditional Szechuan sauce. I make a Szechuan-style broth and serve it with noodles instead of rice (and no-beef of course!). The result is a Chinese/Vietnamese fusion dish that should excite anyone who is a fan of Asian cuisine.

Serves 2

BROTH :
-2 tsp. sesame oil
-I large or 2 small cloves garlic, diced fine
-2 tsp. fresh ginger, diced fine
-1/4 tsp. red pepper flakes
-2 cups beef FLAVORED broth (recommend G. Washington's rich brown broth)
-I tbsp. soy sauce
-I tsp. sherry
-I tsp. hoisin sauce (can be found in Asian section of most supermarkets)
-I tsp. sugar

-2 3 oz. packages Ramen Noodle Soup
-2 tsp. sesame oil
-half of a package of frozen no-steak strips (recommend Morning Star Farms brand meal starter steak strips)
-I stalk of celery, cut into thin, short julienne strips
-I carrot, cut into thin, short julienne strips
-scallions for garnish (optional)

1. To make the broth, heat 2 tsp. sesame oil in a medium pot. Add garlic, ginger, and red pepper flakes and sauté about 3 minutes. Add beef-flavored broth, soy sauce, sherry, hoisin sauce, and sugar and whisk until well blended. Cook on a low simmer for about five minutes. Reduce heat to low to keep warm.

2. Open Ramen noodles and discard spice packet. In a separate pot, cook noodles in boiling water for 3-4 minutes. Drain and set aside.

3. Pour a tiny bit of sesame oil on some paper towel and use it to lightly oil a non-stick skillet. Pre-heat skillet and cook no-steak for 3-5 minutes. Remove from heat and transfer to a plate (don't worry if they are still a little cold). Cut into thin, julienne strips.

4. In same skillet, add 2 tsp. sesame oil and cook celery and carrots over medium-high heat for about 5 minutes (you want them to still be a little crunchy). Add no-steak, stir, and cook for about one minute more.

5. To serve: divide noodles between 2 large bowls. If broth has cooled down considerably, you can re-heat it until hot. Pour hot broth over noodles. If you like, you can strain the broth, but I like it with the sweet pieces of ginger and garlic. Top with no-beef, carrots, celery, and scallions.

Potluck No-Meatball Samosas

Did someone say potluck? That is one of my favorite words my friends! What a great way to throw a party and have your guests do most of the work! It is sheer genius I tell you. But of course, you have to contribute something too. These cocktail no-meatballs are flavored to taste like Indian samosas, and they are out of this world! So make these and make your guests happy. They will still be talking about them at the end of the night. Makes 30

-1 medium shallot, chopped into 3 pieces
-3 cloves garlic, peeled
-3 tbsp. water
-3 tbsp. fresh mint leaves, chopped
-1/2 tsp. cumin
-1/2 tsp. coriander
-1/2 tsp. turmeric
-1/8 tsp. cayenne pepper
-1 dash ground cinnamon
-1 dash nutmeg
-3 shakes black pepper
-1 egg
-1 c. cold water
-3 oz. package potato pancake mix
-18 oz. ground no-beef (recommend 1 1/2 packages Smart Ground)
-5 tbsp. vegetable oil
-1 cinnamon stick
-4 whole cloves
-coriander chutney (an Indian sauce that is usually served with samosas, can be purchased
 at a local Indian grocery or restaurant). Optional.

1. Put shallot, garlic and 3 tbsp. water in a food processor and pulse until you have a paste. Pour into a bowl and add mint, cumin, coriander, turmeric, cayenne pepper, cinnamon, nutmeg and black pepper. Mix well.
2. In a separate large bowl, beat egg with 1 cup of cold water and add potato pancake mix. Mix and let stand for 4 minutes. To this mixture, add the ground no-beef and the shallot/garlic/spice paste. Stir well. Form into no-meatballs the size of ping-pong balls.
3. Heat oil in large non-stick skillet. When oil is hot add cinnamon stick and whole cloves and cook for several minutes to infuse the oil. Remove cinnamon stick and cloves from the oil. Cook no-meatballs in batches for 15 minutes, turning very gently every 3-4 minutes until nicely browned all over. Remove gently and drain on paper towels. Allow to cool slightly so they don't fall apart, and gently insert toothpicks in each one. Delicious served as is, or with a coriander chutney.

Amazing No-Meatballs

These no-meatballs are sooooo good. Crispy on the outside and tender on the inside with loads of flavor. They can make a man want to marry you, they can change a carnivore into a herbivore with love at first bite, they can move mountains of pasta to a higher level. They are, in short, nothing short of amazing! Makes 20-25

-1 thick slice white bread, crusts removed
-3 tbsp. milk
-12 oz. ground no-beef (recommend Smart Ground)
-2 cloves garlic, diced
-1/4 c. grated romano or parmesan cheese
-2 eggs, beaten
-2 tbsp. fresh basil, chopped
-1/4 tsp. red pepper flakes
-pinch tarragon (optional)
-5 shakes black pepper
-1/4 tsp. salt
-vegetable oil for frying

1. Break bread into small pieces and soak in milk about ten minutes. Add all other ingredients and mix well. Refrigerate for 20 minutes.
2. Shape into 1 inch balls. Heat 1/8 inch of oil in frying pan over medium heat. Place meatballs in very gently and fry in batches for 6-10 minutes turning delicately with tongs until they are dark brown all over and can be picked up easily. Drain on paper towels and prepare to be amazed.

"The beef industry has contributed to more American deaths than all the wars of this century, all natural disasters, and all automobile accidents combined. If beef is your idea of 'real food for real people' you'd better live real close to a real good hospital." - Neal Barnard, M.D.

Johnny's Tofu No-Meatballs

These fantastic no-meatballs are the creation of my friend Johnny who is an Italian vegetarian and a very good cook. He refuses to measure anything, but I told him he had to for this because it's a cookbook! I am a confessed ex tofu hater. I think I had a soggy piece once and it left a bad impression on me. Well, these no-meatballs made me do a 180 and I haven't looked back since. Truly, terrifically, tasty. Serve with pasta and Johnny's Quick and Juicy Marinara and you can't go wrong. Makes 20 No-Meatballs.

-1 14 oz package firm tofu, drained
-3/4 c. plain breadcrumbs
-1/8 tsp. paprika
-1/2 tsp. salt
-5 shakes black pepper
-2 tbsp. parsley, chopped (or use dried parsley)
-2 eggs, beaten
-veg oil or olive oil

1. Mash tofu with a fork in a large bowl.
2. In separate bowl whisk together breadcrumbs, paprika, salt, pepper and parsley. Add to tofu along with eggs and mix thoroughly. Form into ping-pong sized balls.
3. Fry no meatballs in 1/4 inch of oil, turning slightly every 1 or 2 minutes, until golden brown and crispy all over, about 10-12 minutes total. Remove with tongs and drain on paper towels.

JOHNNY'S QUICK AND JUICY MARINARA:
-1 tbsp. olive oil
-6 medium cloves garlic, diced
-1 tbsp. dried parsley flakes
-2 28 oz. cans peeled whole plum tomatoes, with or without added basil
-1/2 tsp. salt
-7 shakes black pepper

This sauce is so fresh and delicious, you can put it in a glass and drink it! Serve with Johnny's Tofu No-Meatballs or Amazing No-Meatballs over pasta, or in a no-meatball wedge, and you're in business. Makes enough for 1 lb of pasta.

Heat oil over medium-low heat. Sauté garlic and parsley flakes for several minutes. Add tomatoes, salt and pepper. Mash tomatoes gently with a potato masher until they break down into a nice slightly plump sauce. Stir well. Simmer over medium heat, stirring occasionally for 15 minutes. Quick and Juicy!

Magnificent Manicotti with Red Pepper Cream Sauce

This is a great dish for a lazy Sunday when you have a little more time to cook and you really want to give your family an extra special treat. Total satisfaction guaranteed. Serve with garlic bread and salad. Serves 6

-1 box manicotti pasta
-4-5 tbsp. butter
-1 medium sweet onion
-1 12 oz. package ground no-beef (recommend smart ground)
-5 cloves garlic, diced
-4 tbsp. olive oil
-1 large red bell pepper, chopped
-1 tsp. dried parsley flakes
-1/8 tsp. salt
-8 shakes black pepper
-1 28 oz. can whole plum tomatoes
-2 tbsp. white wine
-1/2 oz. fresh basil, chopped (about 16 large leaves)
-8 oz. mozzarella, chopped in small cubes
-1 3/4 c. whole milk ricotta
-1 c. heavy cream *
-grated parmesan or romano cheese (optional)
* For a lighter sauce, you can omit the cream

1. Preheat oven to 350°. Butter the bottom and sides of a 13x9x2 inch pan.
2. Cook manicotti according to instructions. Rinse under cold water and spread them out on aluminum foil to prevent them sticking together.
3. In medium no-stick skillet, melt butter and sauté onions for about 3 minutes. Add no-beef and cook about 5-6 minutes. Remove from heat and set aside.
4. In seperate, large skillet, start sauce by sautéing garlic in olive oil for one minute. Add red pepper, parsley flakes, salt and pepper. Cook on medium-low heat till peppers are tender, about ten minutes. Add tomatoes and wine and simmer another ten minutes until tomatoes start to breakdown. Give them a little helping hand by mashing them down with a potato masher. Next, add cream, stir, bring to a boil and remove from heat.
5. In a large bowl, mix basil, mozzarella, ricotta, no beef and onions until nicely blended. Stuff manicotti generously with this filling. Lay side by side in one layer in the pan and cover evenly with sauce. Bake for 20 minutes. Serve with plenty of sauce and grated cheese. Magnificent!!

Big Guy Stuffed Peppers

These peppers are comfort food pure and simple. Great for manly men and womanly women. Not only are they good, they are VERY good. The risotto really adds to the "meaty" texture of this filling. But don't take my word for it; make 'em and see. Serves 4

-4 large green bell peppers
-1 10 oz. can condensed tomato soup
-2 1/2 c. crushed tomatoes
-1/4 tsp. oregano
-1/2 tsp. sugar
-1/8 tsp. salt
-1 small or 3/4 medium onion, chopped
-1 12 oz. box no beef (recommend smart ground)
-2 heaping tsp. sour cream
-1 c. COOKED Arborio rice (risotto)
-1 c. shredded Monterey Jack cheese

1. Preheat oven to 375°. Cut tops off peppers and get rid of seeds and white inner rind. Steam peppers for 20-25 minutes until soft and a little floppy (for more "blackened" peppers, fry in olive oil, continuing to roll them over until the skin bubbles and/or turns slightly black. You can also steam them for about 15 minutes and then "blacken" them). Oil baking dish and fit peppers in snugly so they won't topple over.
2. In soup pot, combine tomato soup, crushed tomatoes, oregano, sugar and salt. Simmer for 10 minutes.
3. In separate pan, sauté onions for several minutes before adding no-beef. Cook according to instructions.
4. Mix HALF the tomato sauce in with the meat and add sour cream and rice, mixing well. Stuff peppers with filling and top with a 1/4 c. cheese for each pepper.
5. Bake 25 minutes. Keep remaining tomato sauce warm. When serving, pour a ladleful of sauce onto the plate and set the pepper in the middle.

Righteous Reuben Sandwiches

These incredible Reuben grill sandwiches are so juicy, cheesy, crispy, melty and saucy that they will leave you speechless with joy. You can make big batches of tempeh bacon and leave them marinating for up to a week so that you can eat them over and over again! Serves 4

TEMPEH BACON:
- *1 package plain tempeh (marinate tempeh the day BEFORE you plan to use it)*
- *1 garlic clove, sliced*
- *1 c. water*
- *4 tbsp. tamari or soy sauce*
- *1 tbsp. maple syrup*
- *1/8 tsp. Liquid Smoke (can be found at regular supermarket near hot sauces like tobasco)*
- *1/4 tsp. molasses*
- *1 1/2 tsp. tomato paste*

HOMEMADE RUSSIAN DRESSING:
- *1/2 c. mayo*
- *1 tbsp. ketchup*
- *2 tsp. sweet pickle relish*
- *1/8 tsp. prepared horseradish (jar)*
- *1/8 tsp. vegetarian Worcestershire sauce (can be found easily at your nearest natural food store)*

- *margarine or butter*
- *8 slices rye bread*
- *6 slices Swiss cheese*
- *1 lb sauerkraut drained and heated until warm*

1. Slice tempeh about 1/8 inch thin. Arrange in deep dish. Rub each slice of tempeh with garlic and leave garlic cloves on top. Whisk remaining ingredients together and pour over tempeh so that it is fully immersed. **Leave in fridge overnight.**
2. Prepare Russian dressing by whisking all the ingredients together. Set aside.
3. Cook tempeh bacon in light oil over medium - medium high heat until well done on both sides. Set aside.
4. Butter one side of each slice of rye bread and place butter side down on medium hot griddle or frying pan. Spread a generous portion of Russian dressing on each slice of bread. Top one side with 1 and 1/2 slices of Swiss cheese and the other with 3-5 slices of tempeh and a handful of sauerkraut. When cheese has melted, smush both sides together to form a sandwich and cook until buttery golden and crisp on both sides. Repeat for each sandwich.

Football Sunday Philly Cheese No-Steak Hoagies

This sandwich is everything a Philly cheese steak is cracked up to be: juicy, greasy, "beefy", cheezy, and impossible to eat without taking huge, hulky bites. The carmelized onion touch is to die for! It is sure to make a new faux-meat fan out of even the biggest meat-head in town. Who knows? They might just decide to switch teams. Serves 2

-2 tsp. olive oil
-1 large sweet onion, sliced into super thin slices
-3 shakes black pepper
-pinch salt
-splash soy sauce
-2 large or 3 small portobello mushroom caps
-2 tsp. butter
-1/8 tsp. browning and seasoning sauce (recommend Kitchen Bouquet brand)
-1 package no-steak strips (recommend Smart Strips by Lightlife or Meal Starters by Morningstar Farms)
-1 tub sharp cheddar spreadable pub cheese (Trader Joes or Stop and Shop) or white vegetarian American cheese slices*
-12 inch loaf of Italian bread, sliced into 2 6-inch loaves

1. Heat the oil and add onions, pepper and salt. Cook slowly on medium-low heat for 40 minutes, stirring every ten minutes. Add a splash of soy sauce, stir, and continue cooking for ten more minutes. Keep warm on low heat until ready to serve.

2. While onions are cooking: wipe portobello caps clean with a damp cloth and brush with olive oil. Heat no-stick skillet until hot and cook over fairly high heat for 6-10 minutes until the juices are visible and start to run in the pan. Cut portobellos into thin slices on a plate. Reserve juices from the plate and the pan.

3. In same skillet, melt butter and whisk in browning sauce. Add no-steak strips and cook for 3-4 minutes.

4. Spread both sides of each piece of bread with the pub cheese. Put a generous amount of mushrooms on the bottom piece of bread and pour the mushroom juices on top. Add a heaping amount of no-steak and then load it down with the carmelized onions. Add the top piece of bread. Serve with football. Touchdown!!!!

*If you decide to use the American cheese, you should place it on the bread and broil it in the oven until melted before filling the sandwich with the remaining ingredients. In Philly it is poplular to use Cheez Whiz for this sandwich, but Cheez Whiz is not vegetarian. The pub cheese is a much better vegetarian version.

Beef StrogaNOT

This dish is guaranteed to satisfy the most blood-thirsty of carnivores. Feed it to your meat-eating friends and watch them go back for thirds. When they beg for the recipe, refuse, and tell them they must go out and buy this book! Serves 4

-Half of a 1lb bag egg noodles (the big fat ones)
-1 tbsp. butter
-1 c. onions, chopped
-1 1/4 c. white button mushrooms, sliced into big slices
-2 pinches salt
-5 shakes black pepper
-14 oz. package ground no- beef (recommend smart ground)
-1 1/4 c. clear vegetable broth
-1 c. sour cream
-1 tbsp. flour
-1 tsp. tomato paste
-1/4 c. white wine
-1/8 tsp. salt
-fresh parsley, chopped (garnish)

1. Cook egg noodles according to instructions. Drain and set aside.
2. Melt butter in no-stick pan over medium heat. Sauté onions and mushrooms until tender, stirring occasionally about 6 minutes. Season with salt and pepper. Add no beef and break up into crumbles with spatula. Cook, stirring occasionally, another 5-6 minutes. Add vegetable broth, sour cream and flour and bring to a boil, whisking away as you go. Reduce heat to a simmer and add tomato paste, white wine and 1/8 tsp. salt. Mix and let simmer for approximately 15 minutes or until sauce thickens considerably.
3. Mix noodles and strogaNOT together well in a pasta bowl. Garnish with parsley and let the feeding-frenzy begin!

No-Steak Houdini

Want to know how you turn a standard veggie burger into a delectable Salisbury steak-like entree? Is it a trick? Is it magic? NO no no. It's actually very simple. Just follow this recipe with it's saucy little sauce and you will conjure up a wondrous culinary treat! Serves 2

-4 frozen "meat-like" veggie burgers (NOT garden burgers. Highly recommend Morning Star Farms "Grillers")
-6 shakes from peppercorn medley grinder (green, red and black peppercorns)
-1 tbsp. butter, softened
-3/4 c. water
-1 no-beef boullion packet (recommend G. Washington's Rich Brown Broth which can be found at most major supermarkets in the soup aisle)
-1 shallot, diced
-3/4 c. white cooking wine
-3 tsp. Dijon mustard
-1 1/2 c. heavy cream
-mashed potatoes (optional)

1. Half-cook veggie burgers in skillet two at a time.
2. Grind peppercorns over softened butter and mix until you have a nice spread. Spread on top of each veggie burger and leave to sit.
3. In a large skillet, boil water. Reduce heat and add "beef broth" stirring until mixed. Add veggie burgers and "poach" in simmering broth for a minute on each side. Remove burgers to a warming plate in the oven.
4. In remaining broth add shallots and cook over medium heat 3-5 minutes or until shallots are tender. Whisk in wine, mustard and cream and bring to a boil. Boil rapidly continuing to stir until sauce has reduced and thickened about 7 minutes. Remove from heat and let sit for 5 minutes. Sauce becomes thicker upon standing.
5. Best served with mashed potatoes: Pour sauce over "no-steaks" and save plenty to drizzle over the mashed potatoes. They won't know how you did it!

Mini Mandarin Orange Jello-Shot Cupcakes

I don't think any vegetarian in the world misses Jello. Just the word Jello makes me think not only of ground-up cow hoofs and pig skin, but hospital and nursing home dinners as well. Jello-SHOTS are another story! Jello shots make me think of great parties, and hickeys that no turtleneck can disguise. So here's my spin on an old party favorite. Instead of passing them around as unwieldy, amorphous blobs, I made them into cute mini-cupcakes that you can decorate anyway you like. I put smiley faces on mine!   Makes 24

-1 c. mandarin oranges in light syrup, blended to juice in a blender
-1 1/2 tbsp. agar agar Flakes OR 1 1/4 tsp. agar agar powder*
-1 tbsp. cornstarch
-2 tbsp. COLD water
-1 c. vodka
-One .68 oz. tube of white or yellow cake decorating gel (optional)
* Agar agar is a vegetable gelatin made from seaweed. You can find it at Asian markets, health food stores and Whole Foods. You can also order it online.

1. Line 2 mini muffin pans with mini baking cups. (I use two baking cups for each one, until it sets.)
2. In medium saucepan combine mandarin orange juice and agar agar. Stir and let sit for five minutes.
3. Bring to a boil and simmer, stirring constantly for 2 minutes or until agar agar is completely dissolved.
4. Mix cornstarch with water until thoroughly dissolved. Stir in cornstarch and vodka. Pour into mini muffin cups and refrigerate 2-8 hours until firm.
5. Decorate with smiley faces or whatever honks your horn.
IMPORTANT - These may be little and cute, but they are not as innocent as they look. Don't get too friendly with them because they are strong stuff. Have fun and don't over do it!

Pinky & Eva

Pig-Free

I am in favor of animal rights
as well as human rights. That is the way
of a whole human being.
- Abraham Lincoln

No-Sausage Stuffed Mushrooms
Bacon-Free Cheesy French Toast Sandwiches
Anti Anti Pasta

Zippity-Doo-Dah Chowder
Bang a Gong Wonton Soup

No-Sausage and Pepper Tortillas
Lentil Stew with No-Sausage and Pasta
No-Canadian Bacon and Cheese Grits Casserole
The BEST Half-Southern No-Sausage Biscuits and Gravy
No-Bacon Pie Lucille

No-Sausage Stuffed Mushrooms

These tasty, juicy hors d'oeuvres will make it hard to save room for dinner. They are not the only ones that will be stuffed! If you find yourself receiving shocked looks from your own guests because you have publicly and conspicuously consumed far more than your own reasonable share of these naughty, tempting treats, just assure your guests that there are many more batches in the kitchen. That's what I do. Makes 32

-14 oz. package no-sausage (recommend gimme-lean by light life)
-32 stuffing mushrooms, or large white mushrooms, cleaned *
-2 tbsp. butter, melted
-1 medium shallot, diced
-1 1/2 tbsp. olive oil
-2 tbsp. sherry
-3/4 c. breadcrumbs
-1/4 tsp. salt
-5 shakes black pepper
-8 oz. cream cheese, softened 1 hour
- fresh chopped parsley (garnish)
* You might want to buy extra mushrooms because there is usually a decent amount of filling leftover.

1. Preheat oven to 375°. Cook no-sausage according to instructions. Break up into smallish crumbles and leave to cool.
2. Remove stems from mushrooms by twisting them off so you have nice hollow caps. Dice up stems from ONLY 24 of the mushrooms and discard the rest of the stems. Toss caps in a large bowl with two tbsp. melted butter.
3. Cook diced mushroom stems and shallots in olive oil about five minutes, then add sherry and breadcrumbs, salt and pepper. Cook for a minute or two stirring constantly.
4. Pour mushroom mix and no-sausage into bowl and add cream cheese, mixing with your hands like you would pie dough or meatloaf until ingredients are nicely combined.
5. Transfer caps to baking sheet and stuff each cap with a generous ball of filling so it is nicely mounded on top. Bake 15-20 minutes until mushrooms are juicy. Garnish with fresh chopped parsley and serve hot. Is there a Stuffed Mushroomaholic Anonymous meeting anytime soon?

Bacon-Free Cheesy French Toast Sandwiches

With this borderline rip-off of the classic French dish known as Croque Monsieur, I hope to create a new classic; the meat-free, Mini-Me of Croque Monsieurs, designed to be served as appetizers. They are très magnifique whether served with a glass of Dom Perignon or a bottle of Bud. Makes 15

-1 6 oz. package no-bacon strips (recommend Morning Star Farms brand) OR one 6 oz. package no-Canadian bacon (recommend Yves brand)
-1 egg
-2 tbsp. milk
-1/2 tsp. sugar
-pinch salt
-1 loaf of french bread (baguette)
-butter for spreading
-1 pkg sliced Muenster cheese or Swiss cheese
-2 tbsp. butter for cooking

1. Cook no-bacon according to instructions and set aside.
2. In a medium bowl, beat egg lightly with a fork. Add milk, sugar and salt and mix well. Set aside.
3. Slice baguette into 30 1/4 inch round slices (you may have some bread left over). Spread a thin bit of butter on the top of each piece. Put a piece of cheese the size of each baguette slice on top of each slice of bread. Put a piece of no-bacon the size of each baguette slice on top of each slice of bread and cheese. Take two of these slices covered in cheese and no-bacon and put them together to form a little sandwich. Repeat until you have 15 little sandwiches.
4. Melt 1 tbsp. butter in a large skillet. Dip half of the little sandwiches in the egg/milk mixture, letting the excess mixture drip off a little before frying them in the butter until golden on both sides. Repeat for second batch. Serve warm. Enjoy responsibly.

Anti Anti Pasta

These appetizers are revolutionary party food. Your guests will feel like they are at an Italian meat-fest, but it is all viva vegetariano. My combos are only the tip of the toothpick: feel free to experiment with roasted garlic, pickled mushrooms, hot cherry peppers, salty little capers and/or whatever tastes most rebellious to you! Makes about 50 appetizers or more

-1 box of at least 50 frilled party toothpicks (with the frilly colored cellophane ends)
-1 package no-pepperoni (recommend Smart Deli brand by Lightlife)
-1 package garden herb yogurt cheese (optional), cut into small cubes
-1 jar marinated artichoke hearts, each heart cut in half or in thirds
-1 package no-bologna (recommend Smart Deli brand by Lightlife), cut each slice in thirds
-1 package sliced Provolone or swiss cheese, cut into 1/2 inch wide strips
-1 jar roasted red peppers or pimentos, sliced in small strips
-1 can pitted green olives
-1 bottle of GOOD Italian dressing (recommend Newman's Own brand)

1. For the first combo: fold a no-pepperoni slice in half and skewer on a toothpick, follow with a cube of yogurt cheese, another folded no-pepperoni slice and a piece of marinated artichoke heart. Lay on serving platter and drizzle with a teaspoon of well-shaken Italian dressing. Repeat as desired.
2. For the second combo: loosely roll up a slice of no-bologna and skewer with a toothpick. Follow with a loosely rolled slice of provolone or swiss and a loosely rolled slice of pimento or roasted red-pepper. Lay on serving platter and drizzle with a teaspoon of well-shaken Italian dressing. Repeat as desired.
3. I like to serve this by alternating the toothpick combos on a serving dish and putting a pile of green olives and cubed cheese in the middle. If you like, you can lay out all the ingredients on a platter with a pile of toothpicks and a bowl of dressing for dipping and encourage your guests to join the revolution and make their own anti-anti pasta!

Zippity-Doo-Dah Chowder

This Chowder will put the zip in your mouth and the Doo-Dah in your day. Sweet and spicy comfort soup with a hint of smoky no-bacon flavor in the background that you can savor guilt free! It will literally make you get up and dance. What could be better than that? Serves 5-6

-2 big or 4 medium/baby Yukon gold potatoes
-2 ears sweet corn
-2 tbsp. butter
-3 cloves garlic, diced
-1 shallot, diced
-2 jalapeno peppers, seeded and diced *
-1 celery stalk, chopped fine
-1 14 oz. can CREAMED corn
-3 c. whole milk
-3 c. vegetable broth
-1/8 tsp. cornstarch
-1 4 oz. jar pimentos, drained
-1 tsp. sugar
-8-10 shakes of salt
-5 shakes black pepper
-8 strips no-bacon (recommend Morning Star farms bacon strips)
* Wear plastic gloves when cutting peppers so they don't burn your skin

1. Boil water for potatoes and corn on the cob. Cook both until tender. (Corn will be done first). Drain and cool corn and potatoes. Set aside.
2. In large saucepan melt butter. Sauté garlic several minutes then add shallots, then add jalapenos and celery. Cook until tender, about 15 minutes.
3. Put creamed corn in the blender with 1 cup of milk. Blend until smooth. Pour into large soup pot along with the rest of the milk and the vegetable broth. Add sautéed veggies and cornstarch and bring to a boil. Reduce heat to medium low.
4. Cut fresh corn off cob and slice potatoes into small chunks. Add to pot. Add pimentos, sugar, salt and pepper.
5. Cook no-bacon according to instructions. Ladle soup into big bowls and sprinkle with a generous amount of cooked, crumbled no-bacon. Serve with crusty bread. My oh My what a wonderful meal!!!!!

Bang a Gong Wonton Soup

When I took this soup over to my neighbor's house, her husband, who is a meat-eater, said that it was, and I quote: "The best won ton soup I have ever had!" That's because it is Bang a Gong Soup! (Any T-Rex fans out there?) The supreme dumplings in this soup are easy to make and will leave you feeling quite accomplished as a cook. They also have a lovely hint of my secret ingredient (creamy peanut butter (shhh)). Serves 6-8

** The won tons can be made ahead and frozen in an airtight container for up to 2 months. Thaw before using.**
-8 oz. package no-sausage (recommend Morning Star Farms "sausage links")
-1 heaping tsp. finely diced fresh ginger
-2 tsp. soy sauce (reduced sodium if you can find it)
-1 tbsp. olive oil
-1 tbsp. creamy peanut butter
-1 package won ton wrappers (Can be found in produce section of most large supermarkets)
-1 box no-chicken boullion (recommend G. Washington's Golden Seasoning and Broth) or equivalent
-thinly sliced scallions for garnish (optional)

1. Defrost no-sausages but do not cook them fully. Crumble or mash them in a large bowl.
2. In separate bowl mix ginger, soy sauce, and olive oil. Add peanut butter and whisk until well blended. Pour over no-sausage and mix thoroughly.
3. Measure out 12 oz. of water per serving. For every 12 oz. of water you will need to add 2 broth packets. In medium saucepan boil water and add broth packets, stirring until seasonings are fully dissolved. Keep broth hot.
4. Start water boiling for wontons. Spread out wonton wrappers on work surface. Be sure to cover wraps that you are not working with with a damp tea towel or paper towel so they do not dry out. Have a little bowl of water handy. Put one teaspoon of filling in the center of each won ton wrap. Wet your finger and run it around the edges of the wonton wrap. Fold over like a triangle and seal making sure to push out pockets of air as you go. Fold two corners of triangle down towards each other and seal two corners together to make a dumpling shape. Repeat up to as many as you want. (You need only make about 20-25.) When each one is done place them on an oiled plate to prevent sticking. I recommend freezing and saving the rest.
5. In a large pot, boil won tons in lightly salted water for four minutes. Remove immediately and gently with a slotted spoon. Drain on a plate. (not on top of each other). Ladle broth into bowls and add 5-6 won tons to each bowl. Garnish with a pinch of fresh scallions if your heart desires. Put on some T-Rex for dinner music and get it on!

No-Sausage and Pepper Tortillas

This is simply indescribably delicious. The combination of Italian, Mexican and Middle Eastern flavors just hits the spot. Even if you are not usually thrilled by leftovers from the night before, you will find yourself running to the refrigerator the next day to make sure it is not all gone (watch those untied shoelaces.) Makes a delicious breakfast as well. Makes filling for 4 tortillas.

-1 1/4 c. clear vegetable broth
-2 tsp. margarine (recommend Earth Balance)
-2 shakes salt
-1 tsp. parsley flakes
-1 c. dry couscous
-1 package no-sausage (recommend Boca Bratwursts or Boca Breakfast Sausage Links)
-2 tbsp. olive oil
-1/4 tsp. fennel seeds, lightly toasted and coarsely crushed
-2 tbsp. apricot jam
-3 cloves garlic, diced
-1/2 c. sweet onion, chopped
-1 large green pepper, cut into strips
-3 shakes each of salt and pepper
-2 more tbsp. vegetable broth
-4 large flour tortillas

1. In a small saucepan bring vegetable broth, butter, salt and parsley flakes to a boil. Add couscous, stir, remove from heat. Cover pot and let stand for 5 minutes. Fluff with a fork.
2. Cook no-sausages in skillet according to instructions, but undercook slightly. Slice each no-sausage in half.
3. In large saucepan heat olive oil over medium heat. Whisk in the fennel seeds and apricot jam. Add no-sausages and cook another 3 or 4 minutes making sure to toss and coat no-sausages with infused oil. Remove no-sausages and sauce to a warming plate in the oven.
4. In same skillet add a tiny bit more oil and add garlic, sautéing several minutes, then onions, then peppers and salt and pepper. Cook at least 10-15 minutes stirring frequently until tender. Add vegetable broth and cook another minute.
5. In new tortilla-sized skillet, oil pan lightly with oil on a paper towel. Fry each tortilla 1-2 minutes on each side until golden and crispy/puffy. Re-oil pan for each tortilla.
6. To serve: place tortillas on plates and fill with several heaping spoonfuls of couscous, the no-sausage, and the peppers and the onions. Fold into a burrito like formation and dig in. How yummy is that?!!!!!!!!!!!!!!!!!

Lentil Stew with No-Sausage and Pasta

This stew makes a hearty meal. I even eat it for breakfast sometimes because I can't stop thinking about it from the night before! Serves 6

-1/3 lb. of ditalini pasta (or similar soup pasta)
-4 cloves garlic, diced
-6 tbsp. olive oil
-1 large onion, chopped
-2 carrots, peeled and chopped
-2 celery stalks, chopped
-1/2 tsp. ground coriander seed
-1/2 tsp. dried parsley flakes
-1/3 c. white cooking wine
-1 1/3 cups lentils, rinsed
-2 32 oz. boxes vegetable stock
-8 oz. no-sausage links (recommend Smart Links by Lightlife)
-1/4 tsp. Chinese hot mustard (you know, it comes in those yellow packets you get with Chinese food)
-1/4 tsp. salt
-5 shakes black pepper

1. Boil water for pasta while you chop vegetables. Cook pasta, drain and set aside.
2. In large soup pot, sauté garlic in 4 tbsp. olive oil about two minutes. Add onion and cook about five minutes over medium heat, stirring frequently. Next add carrots, celery, coriander and parsley and sauté another 15 minutes more until nice and tender.
3. Next add the wine. Cook about two minutes. Add the lentils and the vegetable stock. Simmer over medium heat 30-35 minutes until the lentils are soft. (For a more soup-like consistency cover the pot while simmering).
4. Meanwhile, cook no-sausage according to instructions. Cool briefly and slice into disks (8-9 a link). Heat remaining oil in frying pan and whisk in the Chinese hot mustard. Add no-sausage and fry up for about 2 minutes.
5. Now it's time for them all to meet: Add no-sausage, pasta, salt and pepper and heat and stir about five minutes. Serve hot.

No-Canadian Bacon and Cheese Grits Casserole

I became addicted to cheese grits when I lived in the south, and they taste even better with a little no-Canadian bacon and sauerkraut mixed in. A little naughty because of all that butter, but so inviting with the golden bubbly top! Serves 4-6

-3 1/2 c. water
-1/2 c. "juice" from sauerkraut package (when you drain it)
-1 tsp. salt
-1 c. quick cooking grits
-2 eggs
-1/2 c. milk
-5 shakes black pepper
-3/4 stick salted butter
-1 tightly packed c. shredded cheddar cheese
-1 c. sauerkraut
-6 oz. no-canadian bacon (recommend Yves brand), sliced into small strips

1. Preheat oven to 350°. Grease a large casserole dish (bottom and sides) and set aside.
2. Bring water and sauerkraut "juice" to a boil in a medium saucepan. Add salt and grits. Reduce heat to medium and cook about five minutes, stirring constantly.
3. When grits are done cooking, reduce heat to low. Beat eggs and milk together and add to grits. Then add butter, cheese and sauerkraut, until everything is fully mixed and melted.
4. Arrange half the no-canadian bacon strips on the bottom of the casserole dish and pour half of the cheese grits on top. Add the rest of the no-bacon and then the remainder of the grits. Bake uncovered for one hour until the top is nice and golden. Let cool for ten minutes, if you can wait that long (I can't). It's unlikely there will be any leftovers. Once served this dish is usually gone with the wind.

"Vegetarians have the best diet. They have the lowest rates of cor
of our heart attack rate and they have only 40 percent of our cance
years now." - William Castelli, M.D., Director, Framington Heart Study

The BEST Half-Southern No-Sausage Biscuits and Gravy

I am half Southern, and so is this gravy. (FYI, for non-Southerners: this is a classic breakfast dish served in pretty much every diner, and breakfast joint in the south). I replaced the traditional roux with foolproof ingredients so that no matter who's hands this book falls into the recipe should come out great everytime. You don't have to have been making this since the days when soda pop cost a nickel for it to turn out right. I think y'all will love it! Serves 2

-8 oz box no-sausage patties (recommend Morningstar Farms brand veggie sausage
 patties with added maple syrup)
-2 tbsp. butter
-1 cup milk
-1/2 cup condensed cream of celery soup
-1/8 tsp. browning sauce (recommend Kitchen Bouquet)
-1/4 tsp. salt
-8 shakes black pepper
-pinch cayenne pepper
-6 freshly baked old-fashioned biscuits (do NOT use refrigerated biscuit dough.
 Those biscuits are too soft. Use Bisquick mix or Jiffy biscuit mix and cook until well done).

1. Put two plates in a warm oven until the food is ready (milk-based sauces and gravies lose heat very quickly).
2. Melt butter over medium heat in good sized skillet. Add no-sausage patties and cook according to instructions,. 8-10 minutes. Remove no-sausages from skillet and drain on paper towels.
3. In same skillet with the pan "drippings" of butter, whisk in milk, cream of celery soup, browning sauce, salt, black pepper and cayenne pepper. Bring to a boil, whisking constantly. Turn heat to low.
4. Crumble ONE of the no-sausage patties up into very small pieces and add to gravy. Pile each warm plate with three freshly baked, warm biscuits, each split in half and buttered. Spread remaining no-sausage patties out across the biscuits (two and a half each) and smother the whole thing in your no-sausage gravy. Serve immediately.

ary disease of any group in the country... They have a fraction
rate. On the average, they outlive other people by about six
the longest running epidemiological study in medical history.

No-Bacon Pie Lucille

This melt in your mouth pie could easily remind one of a Quiche Lorraine, but my friend Lucille prefers no fuss and hence there is no crust. Don't worry, dearies, it sure won't be missed. At lunch, or brunch, this yummy dish is easy as pie! Serves 6

1 tbsp. olive oil
-1/2 c. onion, diced
-1 clove garlic, diced
-2/3 c. Bisquick
-1/4 c. vegetable oil
-1 c. grated Swiss cheese
-4 eggs, beaten
-3/4 c. vegetable broth
-half of a 5oz. box Smart Bacon, uncooked, chopped into small pieces (about 3/4 c. worth)
-1 tsp. dried parsley flakes
-1/4 tsp. salt
-4 shakes black pepper

1. Preheat oven to 350°.
2. Sauté onion and garlic in olive oil over medium heat several minutes until soft. Cool briefly.
3. Mix all ingredients together and pour into buttered pie pan.
4. Bake 28-32 minutes until fork comes out clean and edges are golden brown. Cool several minutes and serve. Highly, highly recommend pairing this up with a salad covered in balsamic vinaigrette. Good enough to occupy the busiest pie-hole!

No-Killin' Grillin'

*Non-violence leads to the highest ethics which is
the goal of all evolution. Until we stop harming
all other living beings, we are still savages.*
- Thomas Edison

Brian's Portabello Burgers
Grand Opening Chicken-Free Gyros with Ziki Sauce
The Big Stack
Brown Sugar and Cinnamon Crusted No-Bratwurst
Turkey Free Gobbler Burgers
Something to Talk About No-Chicken and Grape Kebobs
Summer Salad with Grilled No-Chicken and Creamy Caper Dressing
Happy Trails No-Steakhouse Dinner
Give Me Mores

Brian's Portobello Burgers

These "burgers" cook up so juicy and smokey and tasty that you'll be firing up that grill every chance you get! When my brother Brian served these up, I practically had to pinch myself to make sure I wasn't dreaming. They are that good. Serves 6

-olive oil
-6-8 large portobello mushroom caps
-6-8 fresh kaiser rolls
-2 avocados, sliced
-orange or yellow pepper, sliced in rings
-1 onion, cut into rings
-2 tomatoes, sliced
-sharp cheddar cheese slices
-mayo, mustard
-salt and pepper

1. Drizzle some olive oil over portobellos and grill them over high heat for 8-12 minutes until they just start to blacken a bit. A couple minutes before the portobellos are done, slice the rolls in half and lay them on the grill so that they get nice and toasty.
2. Create a "burger" by stacking your roll with a portobello cap and any of the above ingredients and seasoning with a couple pinches of salt and pepper (you can slice the portobellos up if the sandwich is too big to get your mouth around).

Yummmy, with THREE M's!!!!!!!!!

Grand Opening Chicken-Free Gyros with Ziki Sauce

Have you ever dreamed of starting your own restaurant? Well, why not invite some good friends over, put up some streamers, and live the dream, at least for a moment, in your own backyard! This recipe could not be more perfect for your opening night. The combination of smoky no-chicken, fresh grilled naan bread, and a super summery, Mediteranean-inspired sauce, will leave your friends feeling like they just ate at the best restaurant in town!

Makes 4 Gyros

ZIKI SAUCE :
- *1 tbsp. olive oil*
- *1 clove garlic, diced*
- *2 tbsp. onion, chopped*
- *1 c. unpeeled cucumber, diced (omitting seeds)*
- *1/2 c. watercress leaves*
- *1/4 c. peeled raw potato, diced*
- *1 c. clear vegetable broth (without tomato)*
- *1/4 tsp. salt*
- *10 shakes black pepper*
- *1/8 tsp. dry ground mustard*
- *2 tbsp. plain yogurt*
- *1 1/2 tsp. apple cider vinegar*

- *4 frozen no-chicken cutlets without breading (recommend Quorn Naked Cutlets)*
- *1/4 c. canola oil or olive oil*
- *1 tsp. liquid smoke*
- *5 shakes lemon pepper*
- *pinch of salt*
- *2 large or 4 medium pieces of fresh Indian naan bread (frozen will do in a pinch) (Can be found at most supermarkets including Trader Joe's)*
- *1 red onion, chopped*

1. Make Ziki sauce at least an hour before you plan to eat. Heat oil in saucepan over medium heat. Sauté garlic and onion several minutes. Add all remaining ingredients except for yogurt and apple cider vinegar. Bring to a boil, reduce heat and simmer, covered, for 10-15 minutes. Puree in blender and then chill in refrigerator at least 1 hour. Whisk in yogurt and apple cider vinegar right before serving.
2. Pre-heat grill to medium high. Wet each frozen cutlet with water and pat dry. In a small bowl, whisk together the olive oil, liquid smoke, lemon-pepper and salt. Use this to baste your cutlets after you place them on the grill. Cook for 12-15 minutes, basting several more times and turning occasionally until heated through. Be careful not to overcook.

3. When the no-chicken is almost done, place naan bread on the grill and sprinkle lightly with water. Cook 3-5 minutes, turning once halfway through. Remove naan to a warming plate and brush it immediately with a little plain olive oil (if you are using frozen naan, thaw completely before grilling or per instructions).

4. To serve: If using large naan, cut each piece in half. If using medium, just chop off the ends of the bread if it seems too large. Slice up one no-chicken cutlet into horizontal slices and lay it on top of the warm naan bread. Sprinkle with plenty of red onion and lots of Ziki sauce. Repeat for each gyro. Fold ends of naan together and eat like a sandwich. You're sure to get rave reviews!

"As I search through my bible today, I find the commandment, 'Thou shalt not kill.' I can find nowhere that it means only human beings." - George H. Westbeau, Little Tyke: The True Story of a Gentle Vegetarian Lioness

The Big Stack

This is so much better than the poor, cruel excuse for the fast food burger that it rhymes with that I double dare you to make it! You will literally feel yourself evolving as you eat!!! Two no-beef patties, not-so-secret sauce, lettuce, cheese, pickles, onions, on a sesame seed bun. And you can have it your way. Grilled, just the way you like it. Serves 4

-8 no-beef patties (recommend Morning Star Farms "grillers")
-8 vegetarian American cheese slices (recommend "Veggie Slices" found in the produce section)
-1 package of 8 sesame seed buns
-1/4 of a head iceburg lettuce, cut into thin shreds
-1 tsp. dried minced onion, re-hydrated with 1 tsp. water for at least ten minutes prior to serving
-24 hamburger dill pickle slices

NOT-SO-SECRET SAUCE:
-1/2 c. mayonnaise
-1 tbsp. Chinese duck sauce
-1/2 tsp. yellow mustard
-1 tsp. pickle relish
-2 pinches salt

1. Fire up the grill as you would for regular burgers.
2. Combine all ingredients for not-so-secret-sauce in a small bowl. Whisk thoroughly and set aside.
3. Defrost no-beef patties until soft. Grill no-beef patties about 3-4 minutes on each side. Place a slice of cheese on top of each patty until cheese starts to bubble and melt. Remove to a warming plate.
4. To assemble The Big Stack: spread bottom bun with not-so-secret sauce. Top with 1 cheeseburger patty, a sprinkle of minced onions, 3 pickle slices, and a small bunch of lettuce shreds. Take another bun bottom (sounds kinky) and stack it on top of what you have so far. Spread this bottom with sauce, and add patty, onions, pickles and lettuce. Spread top bun with sauce and place on top. I think you'll be loving it!

Brown Sugar and Cinnamon Crusted No-Bratwurst

I love wonderfully tasty happy accidents. Like when the syrup from your pancakes spills over onto the no-sausages on your plate. Mmmmm! Well these are just such a yummy mistake done on purpose! The skin on the no-bratwurst becomes this beautiful crusty, gooey, grilled delicacy of seared brown sugar and cinnamon. Delicious with baked potatoes and corn on the cob. Makes 4 no-bratwursts

-1/4 c. brown sugar
-1/4 tsp. cinnamon
-1 tbsp. water
-1 package Boca brand frozen no-bratwurst

Whisk brown sugar, cinnamon, and water together in a small bowl until you have a well blended syrup. Place frozen no-bratwursts on the grill over medium-high heat. Cook on a covered grill approximately 12-14 minutes, turning and basting with syrup every 3 or 4 minutes. Sear no-brats in the final minute by turning the flame up high or positioning them in the center of the flames. Baste one more time before serving. Brown sugar, how come you taste so good?!

"I have from an early age abjured the use of meat, and the time will come when men such as I will look upon the murder of animals as they now look upon the murder of men."
- Leonardo Da Vinci

Turkey-Free Gobbler Burgers

If turkey burgers are the new "healthy" burgers, then these turkey-free gobbler burgers must be the new healthy, HEALTHY burgers. It is time to treat yourself (and turkeys) right! You only have one body and it is not a toy! So gobble these up, and know that you just did something positive (not to mention yummy) for yourself and the universe. Makes 5 burgers.

-2 5.5 oz. packages no-turkey slices (recommend Meatless Deli Turkey by Yves brand)
-1/3 of a 14 oz. package of firm tofu, drained
-1/4 c. plain breadcrumbs
-pinch paprika
-1 tsp. salt
-3 shakes black pepper
-1 tsp. dried parsley flakes
-2 tsp. soy sauce
-4 tbsp. chicken FLAVORED broth (recommend America's Choice brand. Make broth with boiling water and only use designated amount)
-2 eggs, beaten
-olive oil
-browning sauce (optional)

1. Pulse all ingredients except the egg in a food processor until nicely mixed and crumbled. Pour into a bowl and mix in egg. Shape into burger patties.
2. Meanwhile, heat up the grill until nice and hot. Place burgers on the grill and baste first with olive oil, and then with browning sauce. Do not cook in the middle of the flames. Cook 15-20 minutes, turning once, very gently, with a spatula. These tend to be a little fragile during the cooking process. Remove carefully and serve on grilled English muffins. Top with a little mayo and lettuce. If you really want to go all out, try topping them with a good sized dollop of cranberry relish!!

Something to Talk About No-Chicken and Grape Kebobs

You will be the talk of the town, or at least your circle of friends, after serving up this summer treat. Delicious no-chicken threaded on skewers with plump grapes that grill up to juicy perfection in a balsamic-horseradish-honey-mustard sauce. The neighbors will be peeking over the fence to see what smells so good! Makes 10-12 kebobs

-2 9.5 oz. boxes frozen, unbreaded no-chicken patties (recommend Quorn brand)
-1 bunch fresh green and/or red seedless grapes
-1/2 c. olive oil
-4 tbsp. Balsamic vinegar
-3 tsp. Dijon mustard
-1 tsp. grated prepared horseradish (from a jar)
-6 tsp. honey
-1 tsp. lemon juice
-4 pinches garlic powder
-8 shakes black pepper
-several pinches salt

1. Light grill about 45 minutes before you plan to cook. Best cooking time is when coals are just beginning to cool down a bit.
2. Thaw no-chicken patties and cut into kebob sized pieces (about 5 pieces per patty). Alternate no-chicken and grapes on wooden skewers. 1 grape for every 1 no-chick piece.
3. Whisk all remaining ingredients together in a bowl. Line a baking sheet with foil and lay kebobs across. With a basting brush, baste both sides of kebobs with sauce. Cover with foil and leave to marianate in fridge 1-3 hours.
4. Place kebobs on the outer edges of the grill and turn and keep basting as needed for about 6 minutes. Make sure you don't overcook. Remove from grill and baste with the last reserve of sauce that dripped onto the foil lined baking sheet right before serving. Fantastic with rice and sweet corn and salad. Sweet summer grilling success!

Summer Salad with Grilled No-Chicken and Creamy Caper Dressing

This is the ultimate summer fare. Classic and refreshing, and perfect for a relaxing summer night in the old back yard. Serves 4

-olive oil
-2 9.5 oz. boxes frozen, unbreaded no-chicken patties (recommend Morningstar Farms Grillers Chik'n)
-1 small loaf crusty Italian bread, cut in half
-fresh mixed field greens (enough for 4 people)

CREAMY CAPER DRESSING :
-2 cloves garlic, diced or mashed
-2 tbsp. capers, drained and diced or mashed
-6 tbsp. olive oil
-4 tsp. sherry vinegar
-1 tsp. lemon juice
-10 shakes lemon pepper
-10 shakes sea salt or 2 pinches
-2 slightly heaping tbsp. sour cream
-4 tsp. agave nectar

1. Heat grill to medium heat. Place no-chicken patties on grill, and cook according to instructions, about 3 minutes each side. Do not overcook. Slice into medium thin pieces and set aside.
2. Brush the Italian bread with olive oil and lay on grill. Grill until toasty, about 4 minutes.
3. Whisk together all ingredients for creamy caper dressing. Serve each person with a plate of mixed field greens, topped with no-chicken slices, and drizzled with creamy caper dressing. Serve with bread on the side.

Happy Trails No-Steakhouse Dinner

This is a one of a kind camping treat that will re-invent the way you think about cooking outdoors. It is an entire steakhouse dinner with creamed spinach, twice-baked potatoes, and tasty no-steak all wrapped up in one neat, shiny, little package that is pre-made and ready to go wherever you may roam. Perfect for one-night camping trips, tailgate parties, and campfires on the beach. Happy trails to you! Serves 4

-4 large baking potatoes
-4 tbsp. butter
-1/2 c. sour cream
-1 c. milk
-1 tsp. salt
-18 oz. baby spinach
-1 shallot, diced
-2 tsp. olive oil
-1/2 c. heavy cream
-1 tsp. salt
-10 shakes black pepper
-1/8 tsp. nutmeg
-2 tsp. sesame oil
-1 package no-steak strips
(recommend Morning Star Farms steak strips)
-A-1 steak sauce (optional)

QUICK TIP: Use pre-made, store-bought creamed spinach

1. Preheat oven to 400°. Bake potatoes on a cookie sheet for one hour and 10 minutes. Remove from oven and cool for ten minutes. Cut each potato in half lengthwise and scoop the insides out of the skin into a mixing bowl. Add butter, sour cream, milk and salt, and beat or mash until smooth.

2. Cook spinach with just a sprinkle of water until wilted. Drain in colander and press out excess water. Roughly chop spinach on a cutting board. In a medium saucepan, heat oil and saute shallots for 3-4 minutes. Add cream and bring to a boil. Reduce heat to medium and add spinach, salt, black pepper and nutmeg. Simmer for 5-7 minutes, stirring occasionally.

3. Heat sesame oil in a non-stick skillet. Cook no-steak for 6-8 minutes until warmed through. Remove from skillet and chop into bite-sized pieces.

4. To assemble your potatoes: fill one half of the potato with the creamed spinach, and the other half with the mashed potato (you will have some mashed potato left over). Completely cover the creamed spinach side with pieces of no-steak. Put the spinach and no-steak filled half on top of your potato half and wrap tightly in heavy aluminum foil. You want to use about three times as much foil as you need to create a nice tight seal so your filling won't dry out during the cooking process. Store in refrigerator until ready to use for up to 2 days, and a nice, cold, cooler when you take it with you.

5. Cook potatoes in a shallow bed of still glowing coals by your campfire, or on top of the grill, away from any direct flames, until hot inside, about 30 minutes. Turn frequently with tongs to heat evenly. Serve with A-1 sauce sprinkled on top of the no-steak.

Gimme Mores

Vegetarian marshmallows are one of the best things about being vegetarian. Making them yourself is totally unnecessary when there are fantastic confectioners out there who will make them for you, and deliver them right to your door. But enough about that... Look! Look over there to your right! At the picture silly-head! That might just be the most chocolatey, gooey-delicious thing that you ever put in your mouth!

Serves 8-10

-1 or 2 packages vegetarian marshmallows*
-1 box plain graham crackers
-2 large Mr. Goodbar chocolate bars
- Several long sticks or other marshmallow-roasting
   devices

Roast marshmallows over bbq pit or campfire until they start to turn a little golden or stick them right in the flame until they catch on fire. Let them burn a little bit before you blow them out. Either way, make sure they are hot and gooey. Break off a nice big piece of Mr. Goodbar and break your graham cracker in half. Make a hot chocolatey, marshmallow sandwich with the graham cracker on the bottom and the top. Then have some more!

* I highly recommend vegetarian marshmallows by Sweet
   and Sara, which can be found at Whole Foods, or online at
   sweetandsara.com or cosmosveganshoppe.com .

Kids' Menu

You put a baby in a crib with an apple and a rabbit. If it eats the rabbit and plays with the apple, I'll buy you a new car.

- Harvey Diamond, author of Fit for Life

Puffy No-Bacon Cheesies
Good for Your Heart No-Franks and Beans
Nacho Tacos
Chicken-Free Pop Pies
No-Meatloaf Muffins with Homemade Cherry Ketchup
Chicken-Free Parmesan Mini Bagels
Wagon Wheel Pasta Chicken-Free Casserole
Ginger Bread Chili

Puffy No-Bacon Cheesies

These yummy pocket sandwiches are 100% kid tested. Between sighs of enjoyment there have been exclamations of, "This is better than bacon!!" No kidding, kid. You are on the right track. Perfect for a snack or a great dinner served with applesauce and carrot-sticks. Move over bacon, this is yummier! Makes 12 Cheesies

-17 oz. package frozen puff-pastry (2 sheets)
-6 slices colby-jack cheese or American cheese
-12 strips no-bacon (recommend Morning Star Farms "Bacon Strips")

1. Thaw puff-pastry on counter top 40 minutes or as package suggests.
2. Cook no-bacon half of the time that the package suggests.
3. Preheat oven to 400°. On lightly floured surface, spread out puff pastry and cut into 12 squares per sheet. Rip each cheese slice in half. Fold each half over and place in the middle of one square of pastry. Fold one slice of bacon and place in-between folded cheese. Place another square of pastry on top of your no-bacon cheese pile and seal pastry edges together so that it looks like an overgrown ravioli. If it won't stay shut take a tiny bit of cold water and use that for glue. Repeat until you have 12 turnovers.
4. Bake 17-22 minutes or until golden on top and nice and puffy. Cool on wire rack for at least five minutes. Serve warm. Oh, by the way, adults are welcome to eat them too.

Good for Your Heart No-Franks and Beans

In England, where I grew up, kids are practically raised on franks and beans. I sure ate my share, until I became a vegetarian of course. But now, thanks to veggie-dogs, I still enjoy a good old bowl of no-franks and beans now and then, even though I am supposedly grown up. It can't help but bring to mind that lovely kid-song: " beans, beans, good for your heart..." Serves 4 kids

-1/4 c. onion, diced fine
-2 tbsp. olive oil
-1/2 tsp. spicy brown mustard
-1 16 oz. can vegetarian baked beans (recommend B&M)
-4 no-hot dogs, sliced into small round disks (recommend smart dogs)
-hot dog buns (optional)

Sauté onions in oil over medium-low heat about 3 minutes. Add mustard and no-hot dogs and cook another 4 minutes, flipping dogs with spatula. Add beans, mix, and heat until bubbly. Serve in a bowl or in a hot dog bun. The more you eat, the better you feel.

"The eating of animal flesh extinguishes the great seed of compassion." - The Buddha, from the Mahaparinirvana

Nacho Tacos

Are they nachos? Are they tacos? No! They are nacho tacos; a scrumdiddly hybrid of nachos AND tacos. These remind me of my southern grandma who pronounced tacos, "taykos." I loved them when I was a kid and I love 'em even better now that they are made with homemade nacho-sauce and no-beef!!! Serves 6 kids

-10 oz. grated Monterey Jack cheese
-3/4 c. mild salsa
-12 oz. ground no-beef, (recommend Smart Ground)
-1 tbsp. butter
-6 oz. imitation "beef" broth (recommend G. Washington's Rich Brown Seasoning and Broth and use 1 packet mixed with 6 oz. boiling water (OR 2/3 c. clear vegetable broth)
-1/2 of 1 packet mild taco seasoning mix (Old El Paso)
-12 taco shells
Suggested toppings: sliced black olives, pickled sliced jalapeno rings, sour cream, guacamole, shredded lettuce, etc.

1. In a medium saucepan, mix and heat cheese and salsa over medium-low heat until cheese is completely melted. Keep warm on low.
2. In separate non-stick skillet, cook no-beef in butter over medium heat 4-6 minutes. Add broth and half of the taco seasoning packet (don't add water as the seasoning packet suggests). Stir and cook for several minutes until most of the broth is absorbed.
3. Heat taco shells in the oven according to instructions so they are nice and crispy.
4. To serve: Spoon no beef into taco shells until halfway full. Drizzle nacho-cheese/salsa sauce on top and add whatever toppings your kids like. Picky eaters give them four stars.

Chicken-Free Pop Pies

This is a super kid-friendly recipe that gets kids excited about eating their vegetables! These are called POP pies because they are made with enormous popovers that look like balloon bread. They are also smothered in a cheesey delicious sauce instead of that non-descript gruel you find in your everyday pot pie. This is a REAL happy meal! Serves 6 kids

-2 lbs (7 medium) yukon gold potatoes, peeled and chopped into big bite-sized pieces
-1/2 lb baby carrots, each cut once lengthwise and once across
-1 large bunch broccoli, use florets only
-1 box popover mix*
-1 tsp. dried minced onion
-4 tbsp. butter
-4 tbsp. flour
-2 c. whole milk
-1 tsp. salt
-5 shakes black pepper
-3 c. grated cheddar cheese
-20 oz. no-chicken (recommend Quorn brand or Lightlife)
* Popover mix can be found in the regular baking section. Might also be called Yorkshire pudding mix. You will need butter and eggs for the mix. It is sometimes sold only around the holidays. You can substitute canned Pillsbury "Grands" ready-to-bake biscuits, and sprinkle a little cheese on top before baking.

1. Boil potatoes about 15 minutes or until tender when stuck with a fork. Drain potatoes, lightly salt them, and leave to cool slightly. In separate pot, steam the carrots for 9 minutes. Add the broccoli and steam both another 6-8 minutes.
2. Make popovers according to instructions. Add a sprinkle of cheddar cheese to the top of each one before baking.
3. In small cup or bowl add 1 tsp. water to the minced onion. Leave to plump up for ten minutes.
4. In large skillet melt butter over medium-low heat and then add flour and salt stirring with a WOODEN spoon. Slowly whisk in the milk. Bring to a boil and remove from heat. Add salt and pepper. Stir in the cheese until it is fully melted. Turn burner back onto low and stir in minced onion. Let sit on low untill ready to serve.
5. Cook no-chicken according to instructions. Chop into bite-sized pieces.
6. Remove popovers from the oven. Cut the tops ALMOST all the way off so it looks like a little open box with the top still slightly attached. Fill each popover with a nice arrangement of carrots, broccoli, potatoes and no-chicken and smother each one with a generous amount of cheese sauce. If using biscuits, cut biscuits in half and top with vegetables and sauce.

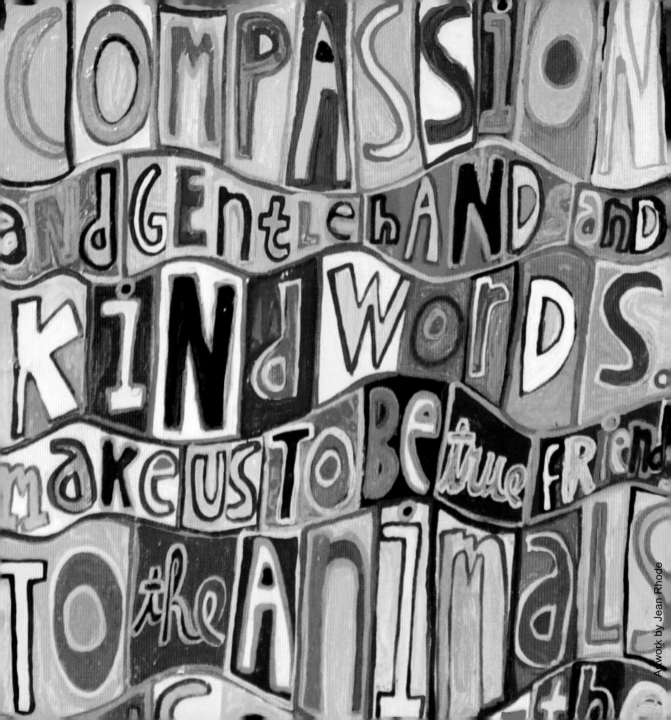

COMPASSION and GENTLE hANDs and KIND WORDS. make us to Be true friend TO the ANiMALs

No-Meatloaf Muffins
with Homemade Cherry Ketchup

These no-meatloaf muffins are made for a kid-sized appetite. Kids love them served in all their glory with my homemade cherry ketchup. The ketchup batch is purposely big enough to leave room for plenty of unbelievable dipping sauce for fries! You can also make the no-meatloaf muffins plain and eat them as is, or slice them up for mouth-watering no-meatloaf sandwiches. Serves 6 kids

NO-MEATLOAF MUFFINS:
- *1 large thick slice white bread (crusts removed)*
- *3 tbsp. milk*
- *12 oz. package ground no-beef (recommend Smart Ground)*
- *2 tbsp. fresh basil, chopped*
- *1 egg, beaten*
- *1/4 c. parmesan cheese*
- *1/2 tsp. dried minced onion*
- *tiny pinch of salt*
- *3 shakes black pepper*
- *1/4 tsp. red pepper flakes (if your kids don't like anything even mildly spicy, omit)*
- *Cooking spray*
- *homemade cherry ketchup (optional)*

1. Preheat oven to 350°. Soak bread in milk for ten minutes. Crumble bread into small pieces and add all the ingredients. Mix gently by hand. Do not pack ingredients tightly together.

2. Oil an oversized muffin pan with cooking spray (the kind that makes 6 big muffins instead of 12 little ones). Fill each cup with equal amounts of no-meatloaf. Press down only a little bit. Again, do not pack tightly. If using cherry ketchup, spread 1 tsp. on the top of each muffin to cover the whole top. Bake for 28 minutes. Let cool for 5-10 minutes so that you can remove them from cups in one piece. Put the rest of the cherry ketchup in the fridge so it can chill while the muffins are cooking.

HOMEMADE CHERRY KETCHUP*:
-1/2 c. red onion, chopped
-2 tbsp. olive oil
-1 c. cannned red pitted cherries in water, drained (about 12 oz.)
-3 tbsp. cider vinegar
-5 shakes black pepper
-1/8 tsp. allspice
-1/8 tsp. nutmeg
-1/2 tsp. salt
-1/2 tsp. vegetarian worcestershire sauce (can buy at any health food store)
-2 tbsp. light brown sugar

* This is a great tomato ketchup substitute if tomatoes tend to bother your stomach.

In small pot, saute onions in olive oil over medium heat about 3 minutes. Add everything but the sugar. Bring to a boil, reduce heat, and simmer about 15 minutes, stirring occasionally. Turn heat to low and add sugar, mixing well. Stir and cook on low several minutes more. Blend in blender until smooth. This is so good you might want to make it in big batches, can it, and eat it with everything!!!

Chicken-Free Parmesan Mini-Bagels

These kid-sized mini-bagels get rave reviews from kids. Sophia had already eaten dinner when I asked her to try one. Not only did she scarf it down with great enthusiasm but she was ready to take on several more as well. This from a kid who said she wasn't hungry! Just be sure to make enough so that you don't have a riot on your hands if you run out! Serves 4-8 kids

-1 10 oz. box breaded no-chicken nuggets (recommend Quorn brand)
-4 plum tomatoes, sliced 1/8th of an inch thick
-2 tbsp. olive oil
-1/2 tsp. salt
-6 shakes black pepper
-1/2 tsp. dried oregano
-1/8 tsp. garlic powder
-4 slices of mozzarella cheese, ripped up into medium squares
-1-2 tbsp. grated parmesan cheese
-4-8 mini-bagels
-butter

1. Bake no-chicken nuggets according to instructions. Set aside.
2. Lay tomato slices on a broiling pan and drizzle with olive oil. In a small bowl, mix salt, black pepper, oregano and garlic powder and then sprinkle evenly on top of tomatoes. Broil on high for about five minutes and remove from oven. Distribute mozzarella slices over the tomatoes and top with sprinkles of parmesan. Broil again for 2 minutes until cheese is melted.
3. Cut mini-bagels in half and toast lightly. Butter bagels while still warm.
4. To assemble bagels: Cut no-chicken nuggets in half and arrange on bagel bottoms then cover with cheesy tomatoes and the top halves of the bagels. Great for kids' birthday parties and similar kid-events.

Wagon Wheel Pasta Chicken-Free Casserole

This dish will make you feel all cozy inside. It has that irresistable comfort food appeal that everyone loves. The fun-shaped pasta and Rice Krispie topping are custom-made for kids. If you are lucky enough to have leftovers, you may hear them beckoning to you from the fridge like I do right now! Gotta Go!! Serves 4-6 kids

-2 cups mini wagon wheel pasta (or regular size)
-2 tbsp. olive oil
-1 medium shallot, chopped fine
-2 celery stalks, chopped fine
-1/8 tsp. cayenne pepper (optional)*
-5 shakes black pepper
-1/8 tsp. no-chicken seasoning (recommend G. Washington's golden seasoning)
-7 oz. frozen no-chicken (about 3 Quorn brand "naked" cutlets)
-1 10 oz can condensed cream of celery soup
-1/2 c. milk
-1/2 c. Rice Krispies
-1 tbsp. melted butter
* Omit if your kids don't like anything even slightly spicy.

1. Preheat oven to 400°. Cook pasta in lightly salted water. Drain and set aside.
2. Sauté shallots in olive oil over medium heat several minutes. Add celery, cayenne pepper, black pepper, and G. Washington's seasoning and cook until tender, about ten minutes.
3. Cook no-chicken according to instructions, chop into small chunks (you should end up with about a cup and a half of chopped no-chicken).
4. Stir together pasta, shallot/celery mix, no-chicken, cream of celery soup and milk. Pour into 1 ½ qt. casserole dish. Bake for 20 minutes. Remove from oven and stir.
5. Mix together Rice Krispies and butter. Sprinkle on top of casserole and bake for five minutes more.

Gingerbread Chili

Dessert for dinner! Is this too good to be true? Instead of serving my chili with boring old cornbread, I serve my molasses-based chili with sweet, spicy gingerbread. It is TOTAL MADNESS!!!! If kids ran the world, every dinner would be like this one! Serves 6 kids

-8 "meat-like" veggie burgers (recommend Morning Star Farms Grillers)
-1 tbsp. olive oil
-1/4 c. onion, chopped
-3/4 c. no-chicken broth (recommend one .13 oz. packet G. Washington's Golden seasoning and broth mixed with 3/4 c. boiling water)
-1 16 oz. can MOLASSES-BASED (NOT tomato-based) vegetarian baked beans (recommend B&M)
-1/8 tsp. ground cinnamon
-1/8 tsp cumin
-freshly baked gingerbread (from a box or homemade)

1. Cook veggie burgers according to instructions. Chop into chunks.
2. Sauté onions in olive oil for several minutes until translucent . Add broth, baked beans, cinnamon and cumin. Stir and cook for several minutes until hot. Mix in veggie burger chunks, cook for a minute more and remove from heat. Serve with big slices of warm gingerbread.

"If anyone wants to save the planet, all they have to do is just stop eating meat. That's the single most important thing you could do. It's staggering when you think about it. Vegetarianism takes care of so many things in one shot: ecology, famine, cruelty."
- Sir Paul McCartney

Celia

Holidays

Be the change you wish to see in the world.

- Gandhi

THANKSGIVING

Bill's Topanga Thanksgiving No-Turkey

Bill's No-Oyster Stuffing

Hallelujah Gravy

Cake Batter Mashed Potatoes

No-Sausage Stuffed Acorn Squash

Harvest Dressing

Brady Bunch Stuffing

No-Turkey with Poached Pears and Wild Rice Pilaf

Tettrazini Kama Sutra

CHANUKAH

Simply Irresistible No-Sausage Potato Latkes

CHRISTMAS

Doodie's French Onion Soup

Sheep Lover's Pie

Lucy's I'll Be Home for Christmas Roast

THANKSGIVING

Bill's Topanga Thanksgiving No-Turkey

There are geniuses and then there is Bill Glasser. This man has dedicated himself to the perfection of the most realistic and delicious no-turkey around. An ever-growing crowd makes pilgrimages to his house every last Thursday in November just to behold and partake in the greatness of his work. I dare any subtle detail to escape him!!! He is a master; from the crispy skin, to the white and dark meat, to the shape and molding of the drumsticks, and he has been kind enough to share this knowledge with all of us. THAT, my friends, is the true spirit of Thanksgiving!

NO-TURKEY:
-1 tbsp. vegetarian chicken powder bouillion (recommend G. Washington's Golden Seasoning and Broth)
-1 1/2 c. hot water
-1 hearty dollop vegetarian mushroom-based oyster sauce*
-1 heaping tsp. Chinese vegetarian BBQ sauce granules or 1tsp. Chinese vegetarian BBQ sauce*
-2 fresh bean curd sheets (also called tofu skin) If you can't find fresh, they also come dried and frozen,
 but fresh is best. These sheets are very large. Not to be confused with the smaller ones.*
-1 soy ham log (dark "meat")*
-1 soy chicken log (white "meat")*
-3 large sweet potatoes
-1 dollop butter or margarine
-1 tbsp. olive oil
-several sprinkles rosemary
-several sprinkles salt
-several sprinkles pepper
-several additional sprinkles Chinese BBQ sauce granules or 1 tsp. Chinese BBQ sauce
- saki (optional for "steady hands")

* The products used for this recipe can be found at an authentic asian market. If you only find soy chicken logs,
 use 2 of those. If you can only find soy ham logs, you can use 2 of those.

1. Preheat oven to 375°. Dissolve bouillion powder in hot water. Add oyster sauce and bbq granules and mix thouroughly. RESERVE 1/2 C. BROTH FOR STUFFING. Pour the rest of broth into the base of a broiler pan.

continued...

2. Open the package of bean curd sheets and remove 2 sheets from the package (they unfold into very large disks).Gently separate the 2 sheets from each other and place them in the broth that's in the broiler pan. Make sure they are both thouroughly soaked in the liquid broth. Leave to sit.

3. Next we are going to open up the soy logs to make room for the stuffing: Using a very sharp knife, slice into the soy ham log, making a small incision about 1/2 in. deep that runs lengthwise all the way down the log. Very carefully, start cutting to the right, following around the inside curve of the log and keeping the knife about 3/4 in. distance from the outside edges at all times. The log will start to peel away from itself. Keep going around, unrolling it with your knife (picture a roll of toilet paper un-ravelling).

4. When you are three quarters of the way done, cut off the last un-peeled section to use for "drumsticks" and "wings". Basically, you are hollowing out the log to make room for the stuffing, and using the hollowed out section for your "drumsticks" and "wings". However, you have to stretch it out a bit first to make it a little bigger. Repeat for soy chicken log. (Bill highly recommends sipping some saki as you work. He says it helps steady his hands. If this was coming from anyone but Bill, I might be skeptical!).

5. Cut hollowed out sections of soy logs into 2 "drumstick" and two "wing" shapes.

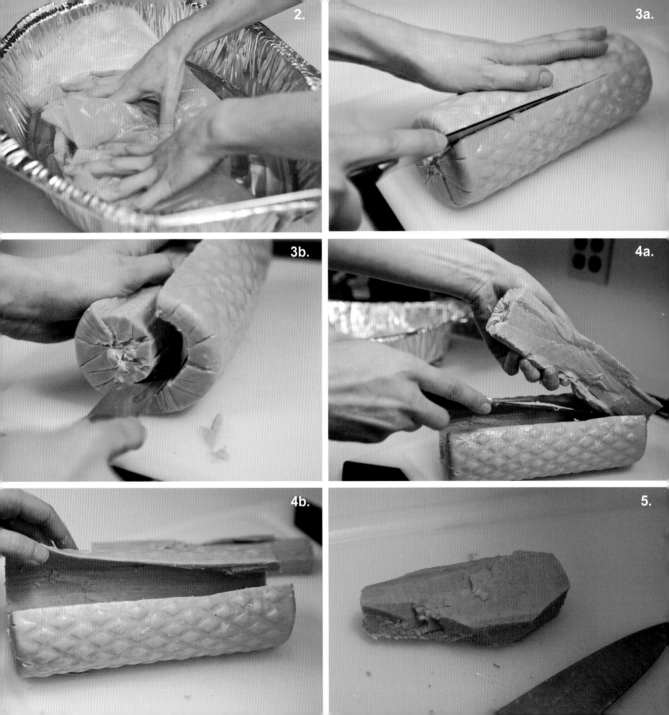

6. Place the unravelled soy ham roll on top of the unravelled soy chicken roll.

7. Put about 1 c. stuffing in the center of the ham roll.

8. Wrap the first bean curd sheet around the 2 layers with the stuffing inside. Cut off a little of the excess bean curd sheet to wrap around "drumsticks". Tuck the rest of the bean curd sheet under the rolled up result. Wrap the second bean curd sheet around the whole thing, reserving a little of the excess sheet for your "wings". Tuck the rest underneath again... a big mass now resembling a turkey!

9. Wrap the reserved pieces of bean curd sheet around your "drumsticks" and "wings". Arrange them around the main body of the no-turkey where they would be anatomically found on a real turkey.

10. Gently cut away the bean curd sheet from the opening hole in the front of the no turkey so that you can see the stuffing. Arrange the remainder of the stuffing as if it is pouring out of the no-turkey.

11 Cut sweet potatoes into 1 in. sections. Saute for several minutes in olive oil and butter. Arrange around no-turkey, and sprinkle with rosemary, salt, pepper, and additional bbq granules. Baste turkey with broth from the pan, and a little melted butter and olive oil, and pop in the oven. Cook for 30 minutes, re-basting once halfway through cooking time. If "skin" has not turned brown after 25 minutes, cook the remaining 5 minutes on a low broil. No-turkey is done when "skin" is golden brown.

(My friend Judy said this no-turkey beat out the real turkey she had this year hands down, and my friend Maureen, after eating Bill's no-turkey, wondered aloud why people even eat real turkeys at all when they could have this instead. Good question Maureen!)

Bill's No-Oyster Stuffing

Any kind of stuffing may be used for Bill's no-turkey recipe. However, except for my own tasty stuffings, Bill's no-oyster stuffing is pretty hard to beat!

-3/4 c. plain seitan (wheat gluten), chopped into small pieces
-2-3 tbsp. vegetarian oyster sauce (mushroom based)
-2 c. WHITE cornmeal
-2 tbsp. baking powder
-2 tsp. salt
-2 c. milk
-3 tbsp. olive oil
-2 celery stalks, diced
-3 cloves garlic, diced
-1/2 c. onion, chopped
-1 tsp. Chinese vegetarian BBQ sauce GRANULES or 1 tsp. Chinese vegetarian BBQ sauce
-1/2 c. RESERVED broth from no-turkey recipe

1. Preheat oven to 400°. Thoroughly coat seitan with oyster sauce. Stir and leave to sit and marinate.
2. Sift cornmeal, baking powder and salt together in a medium sized bowl. Add milk and stir until mixed. Pour batter into an 8x8 greased pan and bake for 30-35 minutes until golden brown. Cool on stovetop.
3. Saute garlic in oil for several minutes. Add onions and cook another couple minutes. Add celery and cook until tender about 10-15 minutes.
4. Cut cornbread into small cubes, or crumble it up until you have 2 cups worth of cubes or crumbles. In a large bowl combine cornbread with marinated seitan, garlic, onions, celery, BBQ sauce granules, and reserved broth from no-turkey recipe. Mix well. Use to stuff your "bird". Happy no-turkey day!!!!!!

Hallelujah Gravy

Bill and I did a little collaboration on this one and it couldn't have turned out better. Eating should be a religious experience, and when this gravy is smothered all over Bill's Topanga Thanksgiving no-turkey, well, it just makes me want to jump up and shout, "Hallelujah!" What can I say? Serves everybody!

-3 c. water
-1 tbsp. + 1 tsp. no-chicken flavored boullion (recommend G. Washington's Golden Broth)
-1 tbsp. vegetarian oyster sauce (mushroom based)
-1 tsp. Chinese vegetarian BBQ sauce
-1 1/2 tbsp. butter
-3 tbsp. cornstarch
-1 c. milk
-6 shakes black pepper

1. Boil water in a saucepan. Add no-chicken flavored boullion, oyster sauce and BBQ sauce. Mix until dissolved and remove from heat.
2 In separate skillet, melt butter and mix in ONE tbsp. cornstarch. Slowly add milk, stirring constantly. Bring to a boil, stirring constantly and boil for one minute. Add dissolved no-chicken broth and 2 more tbsp. cornstarch. Return to a boil, stirring constantly and boil for one more minute.

Cake Batter Mashed Potatoes

What would Thanksgiving be without mashed potatoes? A big rip-off that's what! Now these aren't just any old mashed potatoes. These are such a delicious treat that you will find yourself head-first in the bowl, when you are done, licking it clean as if the contents were cake batter. And don't forget the spoon as well! Serves 8

-5 good-sized yukon gold potatoes, peeled and chopped
-2 tbsp. butter
-10 oz. can cream of mushroom soup
-1/2 c. milk
-2 tsp. dried parsley flakes
-1 tsp. salt
-5 shakes pepper
-1/4 c. canned stems and pieces mushrooms (no salt added), chopped

Boil potatoes in lightly salted water until super soft. Drain and mash in a large bowl, together with all remaining ingredients except for mushrooms. Stir in chopped mushrooms. Serve and lick the bowl clean!

No-Sausage Stuffed Acorn Squash

This is a recipe my mom came up with one night when I was over for dinner. It was so good I told her I had to put it in my cookbook. The squash just absolutely melts in your mouth, and the whole dish is brimming with fall flavors; maple syrup, applesauce, etc. Great anytime, but it screams Thanksgiving to me. Perfect for the main entree or one of many delicious side dishes on what is certainly the biggest American feast day of the year. Serves 4

-2 medium acorn squash (if you are not sure what an acorn squash looks like,
 it looks like an enormous green acorn)
-2 tbsp. olive oil
-1/4 c. chopped onion
-1 14 oz. package no-sausage (recommend Gimme Lean by Lightlife)
-small jar of applesauce
-maple syrup
-cinnamon

1. Preheat oven to 350°. Halve and scoop out seeds from the middle of squashes. Puncture the outside of the skins in several different places with a fork so it doesn't explode on you! Spread oil on a Pyrex (glass) dish large enough to hold the squashes cut-side down. Bake until soft for about 30-40 minutes. If you are using another kind of baking dish, the squash could take anywhere from 30 minutes to an hour and 30 minutes.
2. Meanwhile, in a medium skillet, sauté onions in the 2 tbsp. olive oil until soft. Break up defrosted no-sausage patties and add to the onions. Stir and chop them up until nicely crumbled. Add enough applesauce to bind (approximately 4 tbsp.), leaving some left over for the garnish.
3. Remove squash from the oven and flip them right side up. Brush the edges and insides of the squash with maple syrup. Fill them up with your no-sausage mixture and bake for another 10 minutes.
4. Sprinkle with a tiny pinch of cinnamon and serve with a little bowl of applesauce for people to pass around and top their squash as they please. "Good and good for you," as my mom would say!

Harvest Dressing

This is my Nana's southern cornbread dressing that I dressed up a little more by adding some yellow squash and vegetable broth to give it that extra freshly harvested taste. I can't imagine a vegetarian Thanksgiving dinner without it: The icing on the plate! Serves 10

CORNBREAD:
-2 c. white cornmeal
-2 tbsp. baking powder
-2 tsp. salt
-2 c. milk

-1/2 c. margarine, melted (recommend Earth Balance)
-2/3 c. celery, diced fine
-1 c. yellow squash, diced fine
-2 c. of the cornbread, crumbled
-1 c. dry regular breadcrumbs
-2 tbsp. dried minced onion
-3 c. clear vegetable stock
-2 eggs, beaten
-1/8 tsp. pepper
-1/4 tsp. salt
-1 tsp. sage

1. Preheat oven to 400°. Sift the dry ingredients for the cornbread, add milk and stir until mixed. Pour into a greased 8x8 pan and bake for 30-35 minutes until golden brown. Cool on stovetop.
2. Lower oven to 350°. Take approx. 3 tbsp. of the melted margarine and sauté celery over medium heat for several minutes. Add yellow squash and sauté several minutes more until soft. Combine all ingredients together in a large bowl and mix well.
3. Pour into a greased casserole dish and bake 1 hour and fifteen minutes. Thank you, Nana!

Brady Bunch Stuffing

Do the holiday's bring out the worst in everyone in your family? Do you fantasize about crawling into a dark hole and not emerging 'til it's all over? Sometimes I ask myself, what would the Brady Bunch do? They'd gather around the table and have a golly-gee terrific, hand-holding, belly-laughing time eating this stuffing and so can you. Serves 8

- 14 oz. no-sausage (recommend Gimme Lean by Lightlife)
- 1 c. celery, chopped fine
- 3/4 c. onion, chopped fine
- 3/4 c. green pepper, chopped fine
- 2 tbsp. olive oil
- 1/4 c. raisins
- 10 oz. can cream of mushroom soup
- 1 1/4 c. milk
- 1/2 c. uncooked rice
- 1/8 tsp. red pepper flakes

1. Preheat oven to 350°. Cook no-sausage according to instructions. Break up into small bits and set aside.
2. Sauté celery, onion, and green pepper in olive oil over medium heat for about ten minutes until soft.
3. Combine all ingredients in a large bowl and mix well. Transfer to un-greased casserole dish and bake covered for one hour stirring once half way through. Bake uncovered for 20 minutes more. Gosh-darn this stuff is good!

No-Turkey with Poached Pears and Wild Rice Pilaf

This is a splendiferous Thanksgiving entree. Hearty yet slightly gourmet. Woodsy yet somewhat decadent. Good old-fashioned comfort food that won't let you down! One guest of mine this year was so convinced he'd been eating turkey, he took a "triptophan" nap right after dinner. Hmmmm...maybe it was the whiskey cocktails? Serves 6

- 1 frozen no-turkey roast (Quorn Turk'y Roast or frozen Tofurkey Roast (Tofurkey Roast must be defrosted 24 hours in advance for best results))
- 2 6 oz. boxes wild and long grain rice mix with seasoning
- 4 ripe sweet pears, peeled and sliced around core into big pieces (about 4 each)
- 1 1/2 c. white wine
- 1/3 c. sugar
- 1 cinnamon stick
- 2 tbsp. lemon juice
- 1/2 tsp. grated lemon zest
- For Gravy: Use recipe for Hallelujah Gravy
- fresh parsley (garnish)

1. Cook no-turkey according to instructions.
2. Meanwhile, cook rice according to instructions. Set aside.
3. In a medium saucepan, mix wine, sugar, cinnamon, lemon juice and lemon zest and bring to a boil. Reduce heat and add pears as soon as the sugar has dissolved. Simmer anywhere from 10 minutes to 45 minutes depending on the ripeness of the pears. Turn pears occasionally and cook until soft but not mushy, and until your kitchen smells absolutely heavenly! Leave on low heat.
4. Make Hallelujah Gravy.
5. Spoon the rice onto a large serving dish. Next, spread the pears out evenly over the rice and drizzle half of the pear syrup over the pears and rice omitting the cinnamon stick. Carve the no-turkey into nice big slices and lay on top of the pears. Cover with gravy (you may not need to use it all), garnish with fresh parsley and serve. Splendiferous!

Tetrazzini Kama Sutra

Wondering what to do with your no-turkey leftovers after no-turkey day? You could resort to the usual no-turkey sandwich, or you could really mix it up and make something excitingly different. Don't be intimidated by the list of ingredients; it is mostly spices. Seductive Indian spices of aphrodisiac proportions. This play on the dish turkey tetrazzini brings a whole new meaning to cooking with love. Serves 4-6

-16 oz. leftover or new no-turkey (recommend Quorn Turk'y Roast)
-8 cloves garlic, peeled and cut in thirds
-1 inch fresh ginger, peeled and chopped into medium chunks
-1/2 c. unsalted toasted slivered almonds
-6 tbsp. water
-5 tbsp. olive oil
-6 whole cloves *
-1 inch cinnamon stick*
-1 large onion or 1 and 2/3 cups onion, diced fine
-1/2 tsp. cayenne pepper
-1 tsp. ground coriander seeds
-2 tsp. ground cumin
-4 shakes sea salt
-1/2 pint heavy whipping cream
-3 oz. or 3 little boxes golden raisins
-1/2 c. water
-1 lb cappellini (thin spaghetti) or 3/4 lb spaghetti
-2 shakes black pepper
-dash nutmeg
-dash ground cinnamon
-1/2 c. unsalted slivered toasted almonds,

1. If no-turkey is not cooked already, cook no-turkey according to instructions, but pick the method where you do not have to baste it with anything. Cut into small strips.
2. Meanwhile, put garlic, ginger, almonds and 6 tbsp. water into a blender and blend to a paste.
3. Heat oil in a wok or large pasta pot over medium heat. Add cloves and cinnamon stick to hot oil and cook for about 30 seconds. Add onions and sauté for about 10 minutes until they start turning brown. Remove cloves and cinnamon stick.
4. Add the paste from the blender, cayenne pepper, coriander, cumin and salt. Stir and sauté for 3 or 4 minutes. Add cream, raisins and 1/2 c. water and bring to a boil. Remove from heat.
5. Cook and drain pasta. Immediately add sauce and no-turkey. Toss and garnish with slivered almonds. So good, it just might turn that frog across the table from you into a prince.

* Remove these whole spices before eating.

Simply Irresistible No-Sausage Potato Latkes

Here is a yummy twist on traditional holiday latkes that is sure to light up your table this Chanukah. These latkes are taken to another level of deliciousness. It is simply impossible to have only one. Festively addictive. Makes 20

-14 oz. no-sausage (recommend Gimme Lean by Lightlife which is pareve)
-1 1/2 tbsp. olive oil or vegetable oil
-2 tbsp. onion, diced fine
-1 c. green pepper, diced
-1 6 oz. box potato pancake mix
-2 eggs, beaten
-2 1/4 c. cold water
-2 pinches cayenne pepper
-3 shakes black pepper
- vegetable oil for frying

1. Cook no-sausage in a non-stick skillet until well done and nice and browned (I usually cook it a little longer than the package suggests). Chop up into medium crumbly bites and set aside.
2. Cook onion and pepper in oil over medium heat about 5 minutes until soft. Remove from heat.
3. Combine potato pancake mix with egg and water and leave to sit for 5-7 minutes. Stir in cayenne pepper, black pepper, onions, green pepper and no-sausage.
4. Heat enough oil to cover the bottom of your skillet. Form pancake batter into golf-ball sized balls and drop in oil. Flatten out into pancakes with the back of a spoon. Cook until golden brown on both sides. Drain on paper towels and eat as is or with sour cream or applesauce. Anyway you serve them they are simply irresistible!

Doodie's French Onion Soup

Doodie (pronounced Doo-D) has no French derivation whatsoever. It is a nickname for my dad that was coined by me as a little girl. A Doodie is many things, but for the purposes of this little story, a Doodie is someone who marks different occasions by telling the same story over and over again. And thus, every Christmas eve, when Doodie makes his annual French onion soup, we get to hear the vivid story of how the French meat market workers, after a long day of hacking up cows, would have French onion soup as a poor man's dinner with no meat, just the beef broth, day old bread, and some cheese, and it would warm them up right down to their little blood-stained shoes. A lovely tale, but we have heard it before! And we are vegetarians! And what about the poor cows!? That's why Doodie came up with this brilliant vegetarian French onion soup which compromises nothing when it comes to the taste and makes us much happier (but we still have to listen to that story!) Serves 6

-2 tbsp. olive oil
-2 1/2 c. SWEET onions, chopped into thin rings
-4 10.5 oz. cans clear vegetable broth (or 40 oz. vegetable broth made from vegetable bouillon cubes)
-1/2 c. sherry
-2 tbsp. vegetarian Worcestershire sauce (recommend Annie's brand)
-dash black pepper
-Crusty French or Italian bread, sliced 1/2 inch thick and toasted (day old bread is great!)
-6 slices Swiss cheese
-Parmesan cheese

1. In a large soup pot heat oil and cook onions over medium heat until very soft, but not brown, about 20-25 minutes. Add broth, sherry, Worcestershire sauce and pepper and bring to a boil. Simmer for 30-40 minutes.*
2. Divide hot broth into 6 oven-safe bowls and place on a cookie sheet. In each bowl, float a slice of toast (or 2 if small), a generous slice of Swiss cheese (enough to completely cover the bowl and drape slightly over the edge) and a sprinkle of Parmesan on top. Broil until cheese is bubbly. Serve immediately.
* The broth can be made a day in advance and refrigerated overnight. Reheat before using.

Sheep Lover's Pie

I grew up in England, so I am all about Shepherd's Pie (minus the cute little lambs). My version of this English favorite makes a fantastic winter meal. It is also a fabulous choice for Christmas dinner as it goes along with the traditional "meat" and potato fixin's. I wouldn't be surprised if it becomes a beloved holiday tradition in your house! Serves 6

POTATOES:
-5-6 large potatoes, peeled and chopped
-1 c. milk
-3 tbsp. butter
-2 tsp. salt
-5 shakes black pepper
-2-3 tsp. horseradish (optional)

-3 tbsp. vegtable oil
-1 medium onion chopped
-baby carrots (approx 20), chopped
-1 stalk celery, chopped
-1/2 package frozen baby (petite) peas
- 2 tbsp. butter
-2 packages smart ground (1 1b. each) (or other imitation ground beef product)
-1 and 1/2 tbsp. vegetarian Worcestershire sauce (you can find it at any natural market)
-1/4 tsp. salt
-1/4 tsp. ground nutmeg
-2 tbsp. melted butter for a golden pie top

QUICK TIP: You can always use store-bought mashed potatoes

1. Preheat oven to 400°. Boil potatoes in lightly salted water until tender, about 15 minutes. Drain and mash until moist and creamy with milk, butter, salt, pepper and optional horseradish. Add more milk and butter if necessary. Set aside.
2. In large skillet, heat vegetable oil over medium heat and add onions, carrots and celery. Cook until soft, stirring occasionally, approximately 15 - 20 minutes.
3. Meanwhile, cook peas according to instructions and set aside.
4. In separate skillet melt butter and cook no-beef according to instructions. Make sure it stays moist. If necessary add more butter. Remove from heat. Combine with onions, celery, carrots, peas, Worcestershire sauce, salt and nutmeg. Mix well and transfer to an 8 x 8 ungreased casserole dish. Heap the mashed potatoes on top until the filling is completely covered. Smooth the top of the potatoes. With a fork, make overlapping criss-cross patterns across the entire top surface of the potatoes. Brush with melted butter and bake for 30-35 minutes. Broil on low for the last 4-5 minutes until the top is dotted with golden ridges. Serve and sprinkle with more Worcestershire sauce if desired. Christmas joy and cheer in every bite!

Lucy's I'll Be Home for Christmas Roast

My wonderful English friend and neighbor made this recipe and it is off the charts delicious. You can eat it for days on end and wish there was more. It is completely worthy of being the main entree at any holiday feast, but Lucy's family serves it at Christmas dinner. I would serve it with a sprig of holly stuck on top!* Serves 8

- 1/2 c. lentils
- 1/2 c. brown rice
- 2 tbsp. olive oil
- 1 medium onion, finely chopped
- 2 cloves garlic, finely chopped
- 1 tsp. stem ginger, finely chopped (from a jar. if not available use fresh ginger)
- 10 oz. mushrooms, finely chopped
- 1 tsp. oregano (fresh or dried)
- 1 tsp. basil (fresh or dried)
- 2 tsp. parsley (fresh or dried)
- salt and pepper
- 2 tsp. teriyaki sauce (recommend Kikkoman Teriyaki Marinade and Sauce)
- 1 medium red pepper, finely chopped
- 2 sticks celery, finely chopped (The secret to this dishes' success is FINELY CHOPPED).
- 1 carrot, grated
- 1 zucchini, finely chopped
- 3/4 lbs mixed nuts (peanuts, walnuts, pecans, almonds), finely chopped (recommend chopping in a blender)
- 1 c. plain breadcrumbs
- vegetable stock (only if needed to moisten)

1. Wash lentils, cover with water and bring to a boil. Reduce heat and simmer about 15-20 minutes (until tender).
2. Cook brown rice (or you can buy it already cooked at cool places like Trader Joes).
3. Saute onion, garlic and ginger in a large frying pan until soft. Add the mushrooms, herbs, salt and pepper and HALF of the Teriyaki marinade (1 tbsp.) and cook for about five minutes. Add the red pepper, celery, carrot and zucchini and cook on medium heat about 15 minutes more. Remove from the heat and add the nuts, lentils, rice, breadcrumbs and the remaining Teriyaki sauce. Mix together well. The mixture should be firm. If it needs a little more liquid, add a little vegetable stock.
4. Preheat oven to 375°. Place mixture in a well-oiled loaf pan and press down well. Cover with foil. Bake for 45 minutes. Remove foil and bake for another 10 minutes until it feels firm to the touch. Don't worry if it gets a little dark on top, believe me the crusty crust is yummy! Slice as you would a "meatloaf" and serve with Lucy's cranberry apple Jelly.

God bless us every one! Especially Lucy!!!!!!

LUCY'S CRANBERRY APPLE JELLY:
-3 medium apples, peeled and sliced
-4 tbsp. water
-16 oz. can Ocean Spray whole berry sauce
-juice of 1/2 a lemon

Cook the apples in the water until soft. Add the can of cranberry sauce and the lemon juice and bring to a boil. Let it simmer for 5 minutes and then stir and leave to cool.

*Do not injest holly leaves or berries as they are poisonous.

Little
Dylan

Dairy & Egg Free

I should like to express my absolute horror of the inhumane veal crate! I do hope that compassion will prevail and one more black mark against humanity will be erased. This is a plea from my heart. - Jane Goodall

Pumpkin Waffles with Rum Raisin Syrup and Soy Ice Cream
New Roc City Coffee Cakes
Feelin' Groovy Chocolate Chip Pancakes
Christen's Breakfast Scramble

No-Cream of Asparagus Soup
Fettucine Fred with No-Cheesy Garlic Breadsticks
Mushroom Pesto Presto Pizza
Blue Ribbon Dairy-Free Mac and Cheese
Broccoli and No-Cheddar Quiche

Hot Chocolate Drop Scones
Chocolate Covered Dairy-Free Ice Cream Bon Bons
Steve's Rice Pudding with Candied Pecans and Dried Cherries

Animals raised for meat are not the only animals that suffer in the cruel business of factory farming. Dairy cows and calves, and egg-laying hens, and their chicks, are among the most exploited, and abused animals in the world.

On a dairy farm, cows exist to produce milk for people, not their own babies. The male calves are taken away from their mothers usually within 24 hours of birth, and chained in small wooden crates where they cannot walk or turn around. They are purposely denied any water, so that they will drink the vitamin-deficient milk-replacer that they are given. This does not quench their thirst, but keeps their flesh pale and anemic until they are slaughtered for veal. Because they are denied solid food of any kind, they experience chronic diarrhea, and they have to lie down, and live in their own excrement. The only time they are allowed to walk is from the veal crates to the trucks that take them to slaughter. A lot of the calves are too weak to stand or make this walk, and many collapse along the way. This is the industry standard for the production of veal.

Female calves are raised on a different kind of milk-replacer, so that they can become milk-machines like their mothers. Dairy cows are kept constantly pregnant, and over-milked to the point where their udders become raw and infected. They are kept on routine doses of antibiotics, which are then passed on to humans through their milk. When they are literally, and completely, exhausted of all strength and "usefulness", they are sent to slaughter.

Egg-laying hens are kept in tiny cages with a floor area that is approximately the size of a file drawer. They share this tiny space with 5 or 6 other birds!!!! This is where they spend their entire lives, in a space too small to even stretch their wings. The floors of these cages are made of wire, which causes painfull deformities of the hen's feet. Because the cages are stacked on top of each other, the hens are covered in the excrement of the birds in the cages above them. As if this wasn't bad enough, these hens have their beaks seared off with no painkillers to prevent them from pecking each other to death in their desperation and misery.

In the hatchery, male chicks are separated from the female chicks, and cruelly disposed of within hours of being born. The industry does not want to pay to feed chickens that can't lay eggs and end up as meat on a plate as well. These baby chicks are crushed or suffocated or left to die in garbage cans. All these things you have read above are considered to be legal and acceptable ways to operate in this business. It would seem that whatever concept this industry may have had with regards to respect for life, or even common decency, has been abandoned in it's pursuit of the allmighty dollar.

Baby Dylan shortly after being rescued from a veal crate.

Photo by Derek Goodwin

Pumpkin Waffles with Rum Raisin Syrup
and Dairy-Free Ice Cream

These waffles are sheer decadence. Eat them with just the syrup, or the syrup and the ice cream. Breakfast, lunch, dinner or midnight snack. (Waffle makers are really cheap. I got mine for less than $20 and it works great. If you don't want to get one you can use the batter to make pancakes instead). Serves 4

SYRUP:
- 1 c. granulated sugar
- 1/3 c. rum
- 1/3 c. water
- 1/4 tsp. cream of tartar
- 1 1.5 oz. box of raisins

BATTER:
- 1 c. flour
- 1/2 tsp. baking powder
- 1/4 tsp. salt
- 2 tbsp. confectioner's sugar
- 1/8 tsp. nutmeg
- 1/8 tsp. cinnamon
- 1 1/2 tsp. vanilla
- 6 tbsp. canned pumpkin puree
- 1 c. soy milk (or other milk replacement product)
- 1/4 c. melted margarine (recommend Earth Balance)

- 4 scoops dairy-free vanilla ice cream

1. Make syrup by combining all ingredients in a small pot over medium heat. Stir with a wooden spoon until sugar is dissolved. Bring to a simmer, cover and simmer for 3 minutes. Let sit to cool a little.
2. Sift all dry ingredients together in bowl and set aside. With electric mixer or by hand mix vanilla, pumpkin puree, and soy milk together. Slowly add dry ingredients and mix again. Add melted margarine last and beat until smooth. Set aside.
3. Make waffles in waffle maker. Remove onto plates, dust lightly with confectioner's sugar and 1 scoop of soy ice cream. Drizzle with rum raisin syrup. Satisfaction guaranteed!

New Roc City Coffee Cakes

Think of a doughnut and a coffeecake having babies. These are the babies, and they are yummy, yummy, yummy. If I didn't have this cookbook, I would open up a coffee cake stand on the corner of Main Street and make MILLIONS!!!! But as it is, I am happy letting my friends eat them for free. Makes 8-10 cakes

-1/2 cup sugar
-1 teaspoon ground cinnamon
-2 1/4 cups Bisquick baking mix
-1 tablespoon sugar
-2/3 cup rice milk
-1/2 cup non-dairy margarine, melted (recommend Earth Balance)

1. Preheat oven to 425°. Whisk together ½ cup sugar and cinnamon in a small bowl and set aside.
2. In a large bowl, whisk together Bisquick and 1 tablespoon sugar. Add rice milk and stir with a wooden spoon until a soft dough forms. Sprinkle a rolling board with Bisquick. Place dough on board and knead 10 times. Roll out to half an inch thick. Cut dough with a 2 ½ inch round biscuit/cookie cutter.*
3. Dip each round of dough in the melted margarine and then roll in the cinnamon sugar. Place them on an ungreased cookie sheet and bake for ten minutes. Serve warm (also great the next day if stored in a ziplock bag at room temperature). Millions I tell you, millions!!!

*If you don't have a biscuit cutter, roll the dough into 1 inch balls with your hands and make mini-cakes (makes 20-25). An inverted orange juice glass works too!

"If people knew the truth about how badly animals are treated
these creatures are for their entire lives, if people knew how sever
would be change. If people knew, but too many of us choose to loc
caught in the cultural trance. That way we are more comfortabl
This is how we keep ou

Feelin' Groovy Chocolate Chip Pancakes

What is not to love about chocolate and pancakes? Could there be a happier way to start the day? I don't think so! There are cobblestones to be skipped down, and lamposts to say hi to, and flowers to marvel at! So get ready to feel good, feel great and feel groovy! Makes 8-10 Pancakes

-1 c. whole wheat flour
-1 tbsp. sugar
-1/8 tsp. salt
-1 tsp. baking powder
-1 tsp. ENER-G egg replacer (can be found at health food stores and regular supermarkets)
-1 tbsp. hot water
-1 c. rice milk
-1/2 tsp. vanilla
-dairy-free semi-sweet chocolate chips (can be found at health food stores and regular supermarkets)
-dairy-free margarine (recommend Earth Balance)

1. Sift flour, sugar, salt, baking powder, and egg replacer into a medium bowl. Add hot water, rice milk and vanilla, and whisk until smooth.
2. Pre-heat griddle until good and hot and spray with cooking spray. Ladle batter onto griddle and reduce heat to medium/medium-low. Sprinkle 8-10 chocolate chips evenly over each pancake. Cook pancakes until bubbles form on one side. Flip pancakes over with spatula and cook for about 1 more minute. Remove pancakes onto plates and spread with margarine while still hot. Serve with maple syrup.

oday's factory farms, if people knew how completely immobilized
and unrelenting is the cruelty these animals are forced to endure, there
he other way, to keep the veil in place, to remain unconcious and
hat way is convenient. That way, we don't have to risk too much
elves asleep." - John Robbins

Christen's Breakfast Scramble

This dish is an excellent egg-replacer recipe. Even if you eat eggs, you'll still want to make this because it's that good! Perfect for a Sunday brunch with friends or any old day of the week. Serves 4-6

-3 medium red potatoes (leave skins on)
-1 lb firm tofu
-1/2 tsp. salt
-1/8 tsp. black pepper
-1/8 tsp. ground cayenne pepper
-1/8 tsp. turmeric
-1/4 tsp. oregano
-1/4 tsp. ground mustard
-1/4 c. olive oil
-3 garlic cloves, diced
-1/2 onion chopped
-4 tsp. soy sauce
-25-30 small cherry or grape tomatoes (whole or chopped in half)
-1 oz. fresh parsley, chopped

1. Chop potatoes into quarters and boil for 10 minutes. Remove from heat and set aside.
2. Slightly mash tofu with a potato masher in a large mixing bowl and add all dry spices. Mix well.
3. In a wok or large frying pan sauté garlic in olive oil 1 minute. Add onions and continue cooking another 4-6 minutes. Throw those potatoes in next for about 5 minutes. Add tofu, soy sauce, tomatoes and parsley. Stir and cook another 5 minutes. Let cool several minutes before serving. Addictively delicious!

No-Cream of Asparagus Soup

This mind-alteringly sensual soup has been know to induce happy trance-like states in those who consume it. It is ridiculously easy to make, and so healthy, pure, and untainted, it will make you feel full, and yet lighter, all at the same time. Serves 2

-1/2 tsp. dried minced onion
-1 tsp .water
-1 tbsp. olive oil
-2 large cloves garlic, chopped rough
-1 bunch thin asparagus spears, chopped (Use top 2/3rds and discard the rest)
-5 shakes black pepper
-1/4 tsp. salt, or more to taste
-1/2 teaspoon dried tarragon
-1/4 tsp. turmeric
-2 cups water
-1 vegetarian vegetable bouillon cube (not tomato-based) (recommend Rapunzel brand sea salt and herb vegetable bouillon found at health food stores)
-1/4 c. non-dairy cream (recommend Silk brand soy creamer)

1. In a small bowl, combine minced onion and 1 tsp. water and soak for about ten minutes.
2. Heat olive oil in a medium skillet and saute garlic for several minutes. Add asparagus, black pepper, salt, tarragon, turmeric and soaked minced onion and saute another 5-6 minutes until asparagus turns bright green but is still fairly crisp. Add 2 cups of water and bring to a boil. Add vegetable bouillon cube and stir until dissolved.
3. Remove from heat and ladle into a blender. Add non-dairy cream and blend until almost smooth but still a little chunky (Very important). Ladle into bowls and serve hot.

"Veganism has given me a higher level of awareness and spirituality."
- Dexter Scott King, son of Rev. Martin Luther King, Jr.

Fettuccine Fred with No-Cheesy Garlic Breadsticks

Fred is Alfredo's American cousin. Alfredo likes to cook this dish with heavy cream, butter and cheese which is a little too heavy for Fred. So, Fred made some adjustments and added a couple of touches of his own. The subtle sweetness of the nutmeg and the freshness of the parsley is a really nice touch, Fred. And of course, the no-bacon. Congratulations. Perfectly matched with No-Cheesy Garlic Breaksticks. Serves 2

-8 slices no-bacon (recommend Smart Bacon by Lightlife)
-Half lb. fettuccine
-1/3 c. non-dairy margarine (recommend Earth Balance buttery spread)
-1 1/4 c. non-dairy cream (recommend Silk brand creamer in dairy section)
-1/2 c. non-dairy parmesan (can be found at health food stores)
-2/3 c. fresh parsley, chopped
-8 shakes black pepper
-1/4 tsp. nutmeg

1. Cook no-bacon EXACTLY according to instructions and leave to crisp on plate.
2. Cook pasta in lightly salted water and drain well.
3. Melt margarine in a large skillet over medium-low heat. Add fettuccine and toss with tongs until fully coated. Turn heat up to medium. Add non-dairy cream and toss. Add non-dairy parm and toss. Add nutmeg and pepper and toss and stir until nice and moist.
4. Serve immediately on pre-warmed plates. Garnish with a generous amount of crumbled crispy no-bacon and parsley. Oh, Thank you, Thank you, Thank you Fred!!!!!!

NO-CHEESY GARLIC BREADSTICKS :
-1 sheet frozen puff pastry
-100% non-dairy margarine (recommend Earth Balance buttery spread)*
-non-dairy cream cheese *
-1 tsp. garlic powder
-2 tsp. dried chives
-1 tbsp. non-dairy parmesan
* bring to room temperature for easy spreading or it will go on too thick and tear dough

1. Preheat oven to 400°. Thaw puff pastry sheet on lightly floured surface for 35 minutes. Unfold pastry sheet and spread one whole side with a super-thin layer of margarine, flip over and spread the other whole side with a super-thin layer of non-dairy cream cheese.
2. In a small bowl mix garlic powder, chives and parmesan. Sprinkle lightly and evenly over the cream cheese side. (I usually use about 2/3rds of the mixture and there is always a little left over which is fine).
3. Cut pastry sheet into 9 strips. Twist each strip into a stick-like shape and lay 1 inch apart on a large ungreased baking sheet. Bake for 12-15 minutes or until puffy and golden. Do not undercook. Makes 9

Mushroom Pesto Presto Pizza

Move over French-bread pizza, Here comes some Italian-bread pizza with some real pizza-zaz! Easy and delicious. Make it, bake it, eat it, own it. It's all yours baby. Serves 6

-1 loaf crusty Italian bread, fresh or 1 day old
-olive oil
-salt and pepper to taste
-2 tbsp. olive oil
-12-13 cremini mushrooms, cleaned and patted dry and chopped into thin slices (also known as baby bella mushrooms)
-3 tbsp. sherry
-pinch allspice
-pinch nutmeg
-pinch salt and pepper
-1 lightly packed c. fresh basil leaves, rinsed and patted dry
-2 large cloves garlic, chopped in thirds
-2 tbsp. pine nuts
-1 1/2 c. "mozzarella"-style non-dairy cheese, grated (recommend Vegan Rella or Vegan Gourmet)
- extra basil leaves and/or extra mushrooms for garnish (optional)
-red pepper flakes for garnish (optional)

1. Preheat oven to 350°. Cut off the butt ends of your Italian loaf and slice all the way down the middle so that you have 2 large halves. Brush the tops of both halves with olive oil and sprinkle with a little salt and pepper.
2. Cook mushrooms in olive oil over medium heat about 3-5 minutes. Add sherry, allspice, nutmeg, salt and pepper and cook another 2 minutes. Remove from heat.
3. Pour mushroom mixture into food processor along with basil, garlic and pine nuts. Pulse until pesto-y. Spread this yummy, yummy stuff on top of your two half loaves, cover with "cheese," and a little dusting of black pepper and bake for 5 minutes. Move oven rack up and broil on high about 3 minutes or until cheese is melted and bubbly. Top with garnishes if desired. Presto!

Blue Ribbon Dairy-Free Mac and Cheese

I have a friend who is a connoisseur of dairy-free mac and cheese and she says mine is not only the best but it is in a league of it's own. That is what I like to hear my friends! So I gave myself and my mac and no-cheese a blue ribbon. Let's hear it for the girl! Serves 4

-2 c. elbow macaroni
-1 tsp. salt
-1/2 c. onion, chopped
-2 tbsp. olive oil
-1/3 c. rice
-1 2/3 c. clear vegetable broth
-1 1/2 c. non-dairy cheddar cheese, shredded (recommend Vegan Gourmet)
-1 tbsp. water
-1 1/4 c. rice milk or soy milk
-1/2 tbsp. salt
-1 tsp. dry ground mustard
-8 shakes black pepper
-non-dairy margarine
-3 slices good crusty bread

1. Preheat oven to 400°. Cook pasta in salted water (use 1 tsp. salt). Drain and set aside.
2. Sauté onions in oil about 3 minutes. Add rice and cook 2 minutes, stirring constantly. Add vegetable broth and simmer, covered, for about 20 minutes until the broth has been absorbed. Transfer to a blender.
3. Melt "cheddar" with 1 tbsp. water over low heat stirring until mostly smooth. Transfer to blender along with the rice mixture and add rice milk, salt, ground mustard and black pepper. Blend until smooth.
4. In a large bowl mix macaroni with cheesy sauce until fully coated. Pour into 8x8 greased casserole dish. "Butter" bread slices with margarine and cut into cubes. Arrange bread on top of the mac mixture margarine side up. Bake for 20 minutes. Toooooo Good!

Broccoli and No-Cheddar Quiche

This quiche is so light, fluffy, and flaky you won't know what to do with yourself. My suggestion is to have seconds! Serves 4

-1 1/2 c. broccoli florets, cut into small florets
-1 lb firm tofu, drained really well
-1/8 tsp. turmeric
-1/4 tsp. ground mustard
-1/2 tsp. salt
-1/2 tsp. dried parsley flakes
-1/8 tsp black pepper
-1/8 tsp. cayenne pepper
-2 tsp. soy sauce
-2 tbsp. olive oil
-1/2 c. onion, chopped
-2 cloves garlic, diced
-1 tightly packed c. non-dairy cheddar cheese, shredded (recommend Vegan Gourmet)
-1/4 c. rice milk
-1 frozen 9 inch non-dairy and non-lard pie crust (made with vegetable shortening.
 Can be found at most major supermarkets.)

1. Place large baking sheet on the middle rack of your oven. Preheat oven to 375°.
2. Boil water in medium saucepan. Cook broccoli florets for 3 minutes on a low boil. Drain in colander and then pat dry with paper towels to avoid a soggy crust (very important)!
3. Put your drained block of tofu in a large bowl. Add turmeric, ground mustard, salt, parsley flakes, black pepper, cayenne pepper and soy sauce on top. Mix and mash well with a fork.
4. Heat olive oil over medium heat for a minute. Add garlic and sauté for 2 minutes. Add onion and saute for 5 minutes. Add tofu mixture and saute for 5 minutes more, stirring frequently. Remove from heat.
5. Melt shredded no-cheddar cheese over medium heat in a small saucepan. When cheese is half-melted, add the rice milk and stir well. Continue to melt until almost smooth.
6. Remove pie-crust* from freezer and leave in foil pan (no matter what directions say). Prick bottom and sides of crust with a fork. Arrange broccoli florets across the bottom of the crust. Cover evenly with melted no-cheddar cheese. Top with tofu mixture. Bake in oven on pre-heated baking sheet for 25 minutes. Cool for 5 minutes before serving. Supercalafragalicious!
*For a super-crisp crust: pre-bake pie shell in foil pan on baking sheet for ten minutes. Remove and fill with quiche filling. Bake for 25 minutes more. If crust edges are starting to get too dark, cover them with aluminum foil and continue baking.

Hot Chocolate Drop Scones

Can't get no satisfaction? Look no further. Blissfully hot chocolaty, moist, and melty at your beck and call. Just mix and drop onto baking sheets. No rolling necessary. I think I'm in love. Makes 24

-1 tbsp. non-dairy margarine (recommend Earth Balance)
-1 c. non-dairy chocolate chips (Can be found at health food stores and even some regular groceries like Super Stop and Shop)
-2 c. unbleached all-purpose flour
-1/3 c. sugar
-1/2 c. cocoa powder
-1 tbsp. baking powder
-1/2 tsp. salt
-4 tsp. water
-3/4 c. Crisco vegetable shortening
-1 tsp. vanilla
-1 1/4 c. non-dairy creamer (can be found at regular supermarkets, health food stores and Trader Joes)
-confectioner's sugar

1. Preheat oven to 425°. Melt margarine over very low heat and then add chocolate chips, mixing until melted. Remove from heat and set aside.
2. Sift all dry ingredients into a large bowl and whisk them together. Add water and cut in the Crisco, mixing with your hands until crumbly. Be careful not to over-mix. Add vanilla and non-dairy cream and mix with a wooden spoon until dry ingredients are absorbed. Again, do not over-mix.
3. Drop a tbsp. of dough onto an ungreased baking sheet. Drop a tsp. of the melted chocolate chips on top of that and cover with another tsp. of chocolate dough so that the melty chocolate is sandwiched in the middle. Repeat, spacing the dough drops about a half an inch apart. Make sure the oven rack is in the center of the oven before you set them in to bake. Bake for 12 - 15 minutes until they are fairly solid on top when you poke them. Cool slightly, dust with confectioner's sugar and serve very warm. Come to me, my lovely!

Chocolate Covered Dairy-Free Ice-Cream Bon Bons

For this recipe I am issuing a chocolate and ice-cream lovers alert: If you become overwhelmed by the amazingness of these outrageously good little morsels don't say that you have not been warned. Serve them at grown-up parties or kid's parties, or hoard them all to yourself. I really don't care what you do with them as long as you enjoy them! Makes 35-40 bon bons

-1 pint vanilla or chocolate dairy-free ice-cream (recommend Tofutti brand)
-2 bottles Hershey's or Reese's Shell ice-cream topping*

1. Cover a large baking sheet, or 2 small baking sheets with aluminum foil or wax paper and place in freezer to chill for 30 minutes.
2. Remove baking sheet from freezer and place on countertop. Squeeze quarter-sized rounds of shell topping onto aluminum foil about an inch apart until you fill the baking sheet with chocolate disks (these are for the bon bon bottoms). Return to freezer for five minutes to harden.
3. Fill a large bowl with ice cubes and cold water. Remove baking sheet from freezer and place on top of bowl. Using a melon baller, or very small ice-cream scoop, scoop out little balls of ice-cream and place each ball on top of a hardened chocolate bottom, rinsing melon baller between scoops in lukewarm water.
4. If the ice-cream is really starting to melt,** return to freezer for five minutes, if not continue. Going down the line, squeeze a generous amount of topping over each ice-cream ball, letting it run down the sides. Return to each ball to cover the parts that are still exposed. Return to freezer for 20 minutes.
5. Remove tray from freezer. With the inside curved edge of a spoon, cut away the excess drippings of chocolate from around the base of each bon bon. Peel bon bons away from the aluminum foil very gently and place in the freezer in a freezer bag. Eat when you are in the mood for something too good to be true.

*Smuckers has a shell ice-cream topping but it contains dairy.

**In the height of summer you may want to make these with the freezer door open and the tray still in the freezer..

Steve's Rice Pudding with Candied Pecans and Dried Cherries

For those who think that rice pudding is a rather heavy, and ho-hum affair, I have to tell you, I was right there with you until my friend, and talented vegan chef, Steve Bowe, came along with this fantastic recipe. I am now a believer in rice pudding!!! Steve's rice pudding that is. It is unusually light, exceptionally creamy, and perfectly sweet. The candied pecans are so good, I intend to make them just to snack on. For those who already love rice pudding, I am sorry to say that you may never be satisfied with another rice pudding again. Serves

-1 c. pecans
-2 tbsp. turbinado sugar (raw cane sugar)
-1 c. and 2 tbsp. agave nectar, divided (can be found in most health food stores)
-1 c. Arborio rice
-3 c. unsweetened almond milk, divided (or soy milk)
-1 tsp. salt
-2 14 oz. cans coconut milk
-2 tsp. vanilla extract
-1 c. dried cherries
-cinnamon, for garnish

1. Preheat oven to 325°. Toss pecans with turbinado sugar and 2 tbsp. agave nectar. Spread on parchment-lined baking sheet and bake until golden, about 15 minutes. Transfer immediately to a regular plate before they harden into a stubborn mess!
2. Meanwhile, combine rice, 2 c. almond milk and salt in a very large saucepan. Bring to a boil, reduce heat and simmer, covered, until liquid is absorbed, about 10-15 minutes.
3. Add remaining 1 c. almond milk, 1 c. agave nectar, coconut milk and vanilla extract. Bring to a boil, reduce heat and simmer, uncovered, until rice is soft and liquid has thickened, about 30-40 minutes.
4. Allow to cool for several hours. Serve at room temperature, or slightly chilled, and top with candied pecans, dried cherries and cinnamon.

Veganize-it!

Choosing to become a vegetarian, and to stop eating meat, is a great way to help animals and the environment. Choosing to become a vegan, and avoiding ALL animal products, including dairy and eggs, helps animals and our planet even more!

Most of the recipes in this cookbook can be "veganized", or made without dairy and eggs, and still taste just as delicious as the original version. In this section I recommend ingredients to use as a substitute for each recipe in order to veganize-it!

Chapter 1: Chicken Free

1. Chicken-Free Noodle Soup- use Smart Menu Chick'n Strips by Lightlife instead of Quorn brand veggie chicken.

2. Chicken-Free Thai-Style Noodle Soup- use Smart Menu Chick'n Strips by Lightlife instead of Quorn brand veggie chicken.

3. Popeye's Chicken-Free Salad- would not recommend veganizing.

4. Pasta with Chickpea Pesto- already vegan!

5. Chicken-Free Asparagus Sushi Rolls- use Smart Menu Chick'n Strips by Lightlife instead of Quorn brand veggie-chicken. Use Vegenaise sandwich spread instead of mayo.

6. Cool as a Cucumber Chicken-Free Hummus Wraps- already vegan!

7. Over the Rainbow Chicken-Free Pita with Mango Raita- use Smart Menu Chick'n Strips by Lightlife instead of Quorn brand veggie-chicken. Use plain soy yogurt instead of yogurt. Use agave nectar instead of honey.

8. Cuckoo for Coconut No-Chicken- would not recommend veganizing.

9. Pasta Robino- omit parmesan cheese or use vegan parmesan.

10. From Russia with Love- use Earth Balance buttery spread instead of butter. Use Smart Menu Chik'n Strips by Lightlife instead of Quorn brand veggie chicken.

11. No-Chicken at the Ritz- use Smart Menu Chick'n Strips by Lightlife instead of Quorn brand veggie chicken. Omit goat cheese.

Chapter 2: Cow Free

1. Szechuan-Style Soup with No-Beef - already vegan!

2. Potluck No-Meatball Samosas- would not recommend veganizing.

3. Amazing No-Meatballs- would not recommend veganizing.

4. Johnny's Tofu No-Meatballs - would not recommend veganizing.

5. Magnificent Manicotti with Red Pepper Cream Sauce- use Silk soy cream instead of cream. Use silken tofu instead of ricotta. Use Follow Your Heart Vegan Gourmet mozzerella or Vegan Rella instead of mozzerella. Use Earth Balance natural buttery spread instead of butter.

6. Big Guy Stuffed Peppers- use Tofutti "better than sour cream" instead of sour cream. Use Follow Your Heart Vegan Gourmet Monterey Jack cheese (shred it first) instead of Monterey Jack cheese.

7. Righteous Reuben Sandwiches- use Earth Balance natural buttery spread instead of butter. Use Vegenaise sandwich spread instead of mayo. Use Follow Your Heart Vegan Gourmet Monterey Jack cheese (shred it first) instead of Swiss cheese.

8. Football Sunday Philly Cheese No-Steak Hoagies- use Follow Your Heart Vegan Gourmet Cheddar or spread bread with pre-heated nacho "chreese" dip by Roads End Organics instead of pub cheese

9. Beef StrogaNOT- use Earth Balance natural buttery spread instead of butter. Use Tofutti "better than sour cream" instead of sour cream. Use bowtie pasta instead of egg noodles.

10. No-Steak Houdini- use Morining Star Farms Vegan Grillers instead of regular grillers. Use Silk soy cream instead of cream. Use Earth Balance natural buttery spread instead of butter.

11. Mini Mandarin Orange Jello-Shot Cupcakes- already vegan!

Chapter 3: Pig Free

1. No-Sausage Stuffed Mushrooms- use olive oil instead of butter. Make without cream cheese. Tofutti "better than cream cheese" is very good, but in my experience it does not taste very good when it is hot.

2. Bacon-Free Cheesy French Toast Sandwiches- would not recommend veganizing.

3. Anti-Anti Pasta- use folded up squares of Tofutti brand mozzarella (cheese) slices in place of cheese.

4. Zippity Doo-Dah Chowder- creamed corn should not contain any actual cream and is usually vegan. Use rice milk or soy milk instead of milk. Use olive oil instead of butter. Use Smart Bacon by Lightlife instead of Morning Star Farms brand veggie bacon.

5. Bang a Gong Wonton Soup- use egg-free won ton wrappers (can be found at authentic asian markets) instead of regular won ton wrappers. Use Smart Links breakfast veggie protein links by Lightlife.

6. No-Sausage and Pepper Tortillas- already vegan if you use Smart Links breakfast veggie protein links by Lightlife!

7. Lentil Stew with No-Sausage and Pasta- already vegan!

8. No-Canadian Bacon and Cheese Grits Casserole- would not recommend veganizing.

9. The BEST Half-Southern No-Sausage Biscuits and Gravy- would not recommend veganizing.

10. No-Bacon Pie Lucille- would not recommend veganizing.

Chapter 4: No-Killin' Grillin'

1. Brian's Portobello Burgers - use Tofutti American flavored (cheese) slices instead of cheese.

2. Grand Opening Chicken-Free Gyros with Ziki Sauce- use 2 9.5 oz. boxes Morning Star Farms Grillers Chik'n instead of Quorn brand no-chicken. Use plain, soy or coconut milk yogurt instead of dairy yogurt.

3. The Big Stack- use Vegenaise sandwich spread instead of mayo. Use Morning Star Farms VEGAN Grillers instead of regular grillers. Use Tofutti American Flavored (cheese) slices instead of cheese.

4. Brown Sugar and Cinnamon Crusted No-Bratwurst- use Tofurkey Beer Brats instead of Boca brand.

5. Turkey Free Gobbler Burgers- omit eggs.

6. Something to Talk About No-Chicken and Grape Kebobs- would not recommend veganizing.

7. Summer Salad with Grilled No-Chicken and Creamy Caper Dressing- use Tofutti Better Than Sour Cream instead of sour cream.

8. Happy Trails No-Steakhouse Dinner- use Earth Balance buttery spread instead of butter. Use soy milk or rice milk instead of milk. Use Tofutti "better than sour cream" instead of sour cream. Use Silk soy cream instead of cream.

9. Gimme mores- use graham crackers that do not contain honey (honey is not vegan) like Nabisco Grahams Original. Use a dairy-free dark chocolate bar such as Trader Joe's organic super dark chocolate bar.

Chapter 5: Kids' Menu

1. Puffy No-Bacon Cheesies- use Smart Bacon by Lightlife instead of Morning Star Farms bacon strips. Use Tofutti American flavored (cheese) slices instead of cheese.

2. Good For Your Heart No-Franks and Beans- already vegan!

3. Nacho Tacos- use Earth Balance buttery spread or olive oil instead of butter. Use nacho "chreese" dip by Roads End Organics (easy to find online) or melt Follow Your Heart Vegan Gourmet Monterey Jack cheese or nacho cheese instead of Monterey Jack cheese.

4. Chicken-Free Pot Pies- would not recommend veganizing.

5. No-Meatloaf Muffins with Homemade Cherry Ketchup- would not recommend veganizing.

6. Chicken-Free Parmesan Mini Bagels- use Earth Balance buttery spread instead of butter. Use Follow Your Heart Vegan Gourmet mozzarella or Vegan Rella instead of mozzarella cheese. Omit parmesan altogether or use a TINY bit of Parmazano imported vegan parmesan (easy to find online) instead of parmesan. Use Boca Meatless Chick'n Patties, cut up to fit bagels, instead of Quorn brand veggie-chicken.

7. Wagon Wheel Pasta Chicken-Free Casserole- would not recommend veganizing.

8. Gingerbread Chili- the actual chili is vegan if you use Morning Star Farms VEGAN Grillers. Use the fantastic gingerbread cupcake recipe from the cookbook "Vegan Cupcakes Take Over the World" instead of regular gingerbread.

Chapter 6: Holidays

Thanksgiving:

1. Bill's Topanga Thanksgiving No-Turkey- use Earth Balance buttery spread instead of butter.

2. Bill's No-Oyster Stuffing- use soy milk instead of milk.

3. Hallelujah Gravy- use Earth Balance buttery spread instead of butter. Use soy milk instead of milk.

4. Cake Batter Mashed Potatoes- use Earth Balance buttery spread instead of butter. Omit milk. Make easy homemade vegan mushroom soup: 2 cups sliced baby bella mushrooms, 2 cups water, 1 large Knorr vegetable boullion cube, 1/2 tsp. dry minced onion, 1/4 tsp. salt, 1/2 cup soy creamer. Cook mushrooms in olive oil until soft. Add all ingredients except soy creamer and bring to a boil. Reduce heat and simmer for 2 minutes. Remove from heat and transfer to blender. Blend with soy creamer. Add soup to potatoes as they are being mashed. You may only need to use about 3/4 of the soup.

5. No-Sausage Stuffed Acorn Squash- already vegan!

6. Brady Bunch Stuffing- use soy milk instead of milk. Refer to Cake Batter Mashed Potatoes in Veganize It! for an easy mushroom soup substitute. You will use 3/4 of the soup.

7. Harvest Dressing- use soy milk instead of milk. Use Ener-G Egg Replacer instead of eggs.

8. No-Turkey with Poached Pears and Wild Rice Pilaf- this recipe is vegan if you use the Tofurkey brand veggie-turkey.

9. Tettrazini Kama-Sutra- use Silk soy cream instead of cream. Use Tofurkey brand veggie-turkey instead of Quorn Turk'y Roast.

Chanukah:

1. Simply Irresistible No-Sausage Potato Latkes- use Ener G Egg Replacer instead of eggs.

Christmas:

1. Doodie's French Onion Soup- use Toffuti mozzarella flavored (cheese) slices instead of cheese. Use vegan parmesan instead of parmesan.

2. Sheep Lovers Pie- use Earth Balance buttery spread instead of butter. Use soy milk or rice milk instead of milk.

3. Lucy's I'll Be Home For Christmas Roast- already vegan!

Chapter 7: No Dairy No Eggs- already Vegan!

INDEX

V

Th-th-that's all folks!